The Elliptical Noun Phrase in English

This book presents a detailed analysis of structural as well as pragmatic aspects underlying the phenomenon of noun ellipsis in English. Günther analyses the structure of elliptical noun phrases to account for the conditions on noun ellipsis and those on *one*-insertion, with special emphasis on the (oft-neglected) parallels between the two. She also examines the use of noun ellipsis with adjectives in order to shed light on this under-researched phenomenon, drawing on data from the British National Corpus.

Christine Günther is a research associate at the Institut für Deutsche Sprache in Mannheim, Germany. Holding a Ph.D. in English linguistics, she is currently working on the German language from a comparative perspective.

Routledge Studies in Germanic Linguistics

**Series Editors: Ekkehard König, *Free University Berlin, Germany*
Johan van der Auwera, *Antwerp University, Belgium***

1 **Negative Contexts**
Collocation, Polarity and
Multiple Negation
Ton van der Wouden

2 **When-Clauses and Temporal
Structure**
Renaat Declerck

3 **The Meaning of Topic and
Focus**
The 59th Street Bridge Accent
Daniel Büring

4 **Aspectual Grammar and
Past-Time Reference**
Laura A. Michaelis

5 **The Grammar of Irish English**
Language in Hibernian Style
Markku Filppula

6 **Intensifiers in English and
German**
A Comparison
Peter Siemund

7 **Stretched Verb Constructions
in English**
D.J. Allerton

8 **Negation in Non-standard
British English**
Gaps, Regularizations and
Asymmetries
Lieselotte Anderwald

9 **Language Processing in
Discourse**
A Key to Felicitous Translation
Monika Doherty

10 **Pronominal Gender in English**
A Study of English Varieties
from a Cross-Linguistic
Perspective
Peter Siemund

11 **The Grammar of Identity**
Intensifiers and Reflexives in
Germanic Languages
Volker Gast

12 **Dislocated Elements in
Discourse**
Syntactic, Semantic, and
Pragmatic Perspectives
*Edited by Benjamin Shaer,
Philippa Cook, Werner Frey,
and Claudia Maienborn*

13 **English and Celtic in Contact**
*Markku Filppula, Juhani
Klemola, and Heli Paulasto*

14 **Vernacular Universals and
Language Contacts**
Evidence from Varieties of
English and Beyond
*Edited by Markku Filppula,
Juhani Klemola, and Heli
Paulasto*

15 **Reciprocity in English**
Historical Development and
Synchronic Structure
Florian Haas

16 **The Elliptical Noun Phrase
in English**
Structure and Use
Christine Günther

The Elliptical Noun Phrase in English

Structure and Use

Christine Günther

Routledge
Taylor & Francis Group
NEW YORK AND LONDON

First published 2013
by Routledge
711 Third Avenue, New York, NY 10017

Simultaneously published in the UK
by Routledge
2 Park Square, Milton Park, Abingdon, Oxfordshire OX14 4RN

First issued in paperback 2015

Routledge is an imprint of the Taylor & Francis Group,
an informa business

© 2013 Taylor & Francis

The right of Christine Günther to be identified as author of this work has
been asserted by him/her in accordance with sections 77 and 78 of the
Copyright, Designs and Patents Act 1988.

All rights reserved. No part of this book may be reprinted or reproduced or
utilised in any form or by any electronic, mechanical, or other means, now
known or hereafter invented, including photocopying and recording, or in
any information storage or retrieval system, without permission in writing
from the publishers.

Trademark Notice: Product or corporate names may be trademarks or
registered trademarks, and are used only for identification and explanation
without intent to infringe.

Library of Congress Cataloging-in-Publication Data

Günther, Christine, 1981–
   The elliptical noun phrase in English : structure and use / by Christine
Gunther.
      p. cm. — (Routledge Studies in Germanic Linguistics; 16)
   Includes bibliographical references and index.
1. Grammar, Comparative and general—Ellipsis. 2. English language—
Noun phrase. 3. German language—Noun phrase.
4. Comparison (Grammar) 5. German language—Grammar,
Comparative—English. 6. English language—Grammar,
Comparative—German. 7. Comparison (Grammar)
8. Grammar, Comparative and general—Syntax. I. Title.
  P291.3.G86 2012
  425'.5—dc23
  2012025377

ISBN 13: 978-1-138-92276-1 (pbk)
ISBN 13: 978-0-415-65826-3 (hbk)

Typeset in Sabon
by Apex CoVantage, LLC

For my parents and my sister

Contents

Acknowledgments	xi
1 Introduction	**1**
1.1 Nounless Noun Phrases	1
1.2 Aims and Scope	2
1.3 Theoretical Background and Terminology	4
2 Licensors of Empty Nouns in English—Setting the Scene	**8**
2.1 Licensors of Noun Ellipsis in English	8
2.1.1 Overview of Prenominal Items and the Heads They Take	8
2.1.2 Determiners	9
2.1.3 Adjectives	11
2.2 Noun Ellipsis in German	12
2.3 Questions to Be Addressed	19
3 Inflection, Focus, and Partitivity—Previous Accounts of Noun Ellipsis	**21**
3.1 Two Empty Nouns and Their Properties	21
3.2 Inflection and Agreement	25
3.2.1 Lobeck's Analysis	26
3.2.2 Kester's Analysis	27
3.2.3 Against Formal Licensing and Identification	29
3.3 Semantic Features—Partitivity	30
3.3.1 Sleeman's (1996) Account for Noun Ellipsis	30
3.3.2 The Notion of Partitivity	33
3.3.2.1 *The Syntactic Definition of Partitivity*	33
3.3.2.2 *Partitivity as a Semantic Feature*	35

viii *Contents*

3.4 Information Structure	39
3.4.1 Focus Projections	40
3.4.2 Semantic Effects of Focus	42
3.5 *One* as a Classifier	44
3.6 Summary	45

4 Conditions on Noun Ellipsis in English   **48**

4.1 Empty Nouns and Contrast	48
4.2 Noun Ellipsis versus *One*-Insertion	55
4.2.1 Mass-Count Properties of the Licensors	57
4.2.2 The Nature of *Every One*	59
4.2.3 Some Remarks on the Definite Article	63
4.3 The Structure of the Elliptical Noun Phrase	66
4.3.1 Deletion Under Adjacency	69
4.3.2 Nominal Classification and Ellipsis	72
4.3.2.1 *Different Nominal Classification Systems*	73
4.3.2.2 *Noun Ellipsis and the Mass-Count Distinction in English*	74
4.3.2.3 *Non–Antecedent-Based Uses of Empty Nouns*	76
4.3.2.4 *Noun Ellipsis in German*	78
4.4 Summary	83

5 Adjectival Modifiers in Elliptical Noun Phrases   **85**

5.1 Conducting a Corpus Study on Noun Ellipsis	86
5.2 Adjectives Used in Elliptical Noun Phrases	91
5.3 Contextual Limitations of Sets: Taxonomies and Lexical Relations	95
5.3.1 Different Uses of Elliptical Noun Phrases	95
5.3.1.1 *Taxonomizing Contexts*	95
5.3.1.2 *Lexical Relations*	98
5.3.1.3 *Further Means to Express Contrast*	101
5.3.2 Contextual Limitations of Reference Sets	103
5.3.2.1 *The Notion of Classifying Adjectives*	103
5.3.2.2 *Closed Sets of Referents*	105
5.4 Preference for Elliptical Noun Phrases in Taxonomies	106
5.4.1 Realizations of the Head Noun: Lexical, Silent, and *One*	107
5.4.2 Distance between Anaphor and Antecedent	111

Contents ix

5.4.3 Text Types	113
5.4.4 Antecedents of the Silent Noun and *One*	114
5.4.5 Generic Reference	116
5.5 Accessibility	118
5.5.1 Anaphoric Head Noun Realizations with *Old* and *New*	119
5.5.2 Factors Determining Accessibility	124
5.6 Summary and Conclusion	126

6 Summary   **129**

Notes	133
References	145
Index	151

Acknowledgments

This study is based on my doctoral dissertation, defended at the University of Osnabrück in 2011. I owe thanks to three anonymous reviewers for helpful comments that contributed significantly to the revision of the original material.

These acknowledgments certainly cannot do justice to all the people who have supported me in one way or another, accompanying me through several stages of my work, but I will try to address as many of them as possible.

The interest in the English noun phrase was initiated in my second year as an undergraduate student at the University of Düsseldorf, when I took a class given by Anette Rosenbach, which had a considerable share in my decision to focus on linguistics in general and the nominal domain in particular. I am very grateful to Anette for her inspiration and constant support. I am also thankful to Dieter Stein and the (former) staff of the Department of English Language and Linguistics at the University of Düsseldorf for my pleasant and inspiring time as a student assistant.

When I took up my dissertation project, I soon realized that I needed a reliable set of data. My supervisor, Alexander Bergs, and my colleague Lena Heine suggested using corpora to clarify the matter. Up to that point, I was admittedly skeptical of that method, and, at first glance, my doubts were confirmed—I spent weeks working through thousands of examples to pick out the ones that met my definition of noun ellipsis. But I revised my attitude toward corpora because they gave me a profound set of data I would not have received otherwise. I am thankful to both Alex and Lena for this suggestion and their support throughout my time at the English Department of the University of Osnabrück. I also owe thanks to my colleagues Verena Barbosa Duarte and Meike Pfaff for enduring (and enjoying) the ups and downs of being PhD students together, and to Verena and Mina and Nicky Vollstedt for providing shelter.

I am also indebted to the many colleagues who made helpful suggestions at various conferences (NP 1 and 2, ICLCE 3 and 4, ISLE 2)—there are simply too many to name here. Special thanks goes to Gisela Zifonun and my colleagues at Institut für Deutsche Sprache in the Grammatik des Deutschen im Europäischen Vergleich project. The cooperation within this xii *Acknowledgments*

project contributed enormously to the present form of the study. Furthermore, I would like to thank Carola Trips and the staff at the Department for Diachronic English Linguistics for inspiring discussions and for making sure I do not lose touch with English linguistics.

This book would not have been possible without Dennis Ott, who never tired of answering my questions and of discussing the same aspects over and over again. I am deeply indebted to Dennis for his support, his friendship, and his belief in me.

Last, but not least, I would like to express my gratitude to my parents, Sabine and Horst Günther, my sister, Julia Günther, as well as my friends Nina Delvos, Susanne Erhardt, Svenja König, Uta Koppert-Maats, Zoe Karastogianni, Steffie Mehlem, and Anna Volodina for support in every possible way.

Mannheim, 14 May 2012
Christine Günther

1   Introduction

1.1 NOUNLESS NOUN PHRASES

In the English language, there are a number of nominal constructions that do not require a lexical nominal head. This is obvious with respect to nonlexical nominal elements that either replace the whole noun phrase, as in example (1), or parts of the phrase, as in example (2):

(1) When <u>the headmaster</u> saw the damage, **he** called in the police. (Stirling & Huddleston 2002: 1455)

(2) I asked for a <u>key</u> but he gave me the wrong **one**. (ibid.: 1511)

In example (1), the noun phrase *the headmaster* is substituted by a personal pronoun; in example (2), the noun *key* is substituted by the noun *one*.[1] The latter strategy, which will play a major role in subsequent chapters, will be referred to as *one*-insertion.[2]

Apart from these substitution or replacement strategies, there are also instances of noun phrases that do not contain any nominal element at all. This is evident in the following examples:

(3) While Kim had lots of books, Pat had **very few**. (Payne & Huddleston 2002: 411)

(4) **Few** of her friends knew she was ill. (ibid.)

(5) **The rich** cannot enter the kingdom of Heaven. (ibid.: 417)

(6) We are going to attempt **the utterly impossible**. (ibid.)

Example (3) illustrates an instance of noun ellipsis (also called nominal ellipsis, see, e.g., Eguren 2010, or noun phrase ellipsis, see, e.g., Corver & van Koppen 2009—depending on the type of framework). The noun phrase *very few* lacks a nominal head, but the contents of this "missing" noun is recoverable with the help of the antecedent provided in the subordinate clause. Similarly,

2 The Elliptical Noun Phrase in English

the noun phrase *few* as part of the partitive construction *few of her friends* is interpretable, because the prepositional phrase renders the lexical contents.

Examples (5) and (6), however, differ from noun ellipsis and the partitive construction in that no lexical noun in the context is required for the interpretation. *The rich* generically refers to rich people, and the construction will thus be called the Human Construction. The meaning of the phrase in example (6) can be paraphrased as "that which is utterly impossible" (Payne & Huddleston 2002: 418), that is, it refers to something abstract. This is why this nounless noun phrase is labeled Abstract Construction (see also Kester 1996a; Günther 2012).

A question that arises naturally at this point is why these examples are not treated as instances of adjective-to-noun conversion, as suggested by some authors (see, e.g., Bauer 1983: 230; Giannakidou & Stavrou 1999; Plag 2003: 108). As Payne and Huddleston (2002: 418) point out, these modifiers retain their adjectival properties: They do not undergo plural inflection (see also Olsen 1987; Panagiotidis 2002: 56; Günther 2012; Günther, forthcoming), and they can take adverbial modifiers, as evident in example (6). The same holds for cases of noun ellipsis and the partitive construction: There is no plural inflection on the elements, and they can be modified by adverbials, as can be seen in example (3).

1.2 AIMS AND SCOPE

This work sets out to analyze the structure of noun phrases without nouns and their use. The focus will be on elliptical noun phrases and *one*-insertion, but the other types of phrases mentioned above will be taken into consideration as well. The main questions center on the conditions of noun ellipsis, comprising aspects such as the type of elements that license noun ellipsis, their common properties, the relation between *one*-insertion and noun ellipsis, and the question of which contexts the noun can be omitted.

Even though the focus in this work will be on the English language, nounless noun phrases in German will be given consideration in order to point out how language-specific differences relate to different inflectional systems. Because a full-fledged analysis of the conditions on noun ellipsis in German is beyond the scope of this work, only the main aspects will be summarized to provide a reference-point for the phenomena in English.

As points of departure with respect to data, Huddleston and Pullum (2002) and in particular Payne and Huddleston's (2002) chapter on nouns and noun phrases as well as Stirling and Huddleston's (2002) chapter on deixis and anaphora were chosen, because they contain a detailed description of the "fused-head construction," which is corresponding to what has been labeled "nounless noun phrases" here, and the use of nominal *one* in English. However, this merely serves as a starting point to outline the questions that arise. The analysis presented will be backed up by corpus data.

Introduction 3

The use of corpora is motivated by a range of aspects. First, as will become evident in Chapter 2, it is partly controversial as to which elements allow for noun ellipsis. Whereas matters are more straightforward with regard to determiners, it is far from clear whether adjectives that denote properties can be used without a nominal head in anaphoric (i.e., elliptical) contexts,[3] which constraints apply, and whether these restrictions are of semantic, pragmatic, or syntactic nature.

In order to determine the types of adjectives that occur in this construction, it is essential to have a look at naturally occurring language use. Elicitation, the testing of previously constructed examples with native speakers— although definitely appropriate for tackling some questions—only offers a limited range of options, because only a smaller number of representatives of each adjectival class can be checked. As researchers can only test what they have been anticipating, some interesting aspects that might be helpful to get a broader picture of the phenomenon might simply remain unnoticed. Furthermore, as the controversies with regard to adjectival licensors, to be outlined in Chapter 2, demonstrate, native speakers' intuitions are not always reliable, especially if the phenomenon under scrutiny is rather marginal and a borderline case in terms of grammaticality judgments. In addition, to gain deeper insights into pragmatic factors that might be relevant for the use of adjectives in elliptical noun phrases, such as accessibility (see Ariel 1990, who used text samples for her seminal work on discourse reference), a corpus study offers a wider range of opportunities, because corpora provide linguistic phenomena with their authentic co-texts and contexts.

Using corpus data to shed light on the structure and the use of the English noun phrase is common practice (see, e.g., the contributions in González-Álvarez et al. 2011). The study by Keizer (2007) demonstrates the merits of corpus data for the analysis of nominal structures. It is worthwhile to emphasize at this point that the present analysis is not to be understood as a corpus linguistic study in the stricter sense. It is meant to provide insights into the phenomenon of nounless noun phrases by presenting authentic examples rather than statistical analyses of the aspects under scrutiny; that is, the study is qualitative rather than quantitative, or, in the words of Tognini-Bonelli (2001), it is "corpus-based" rather than "corpus-driven."

For the main study, the *British National Corpus* (BNC) was selected. It is a 100-million-word text collection comprising both spoken (10%) and written texts (90%), covering a wide range of different types (transcripts from informal conversations, fiction, newspaper articles, and academic books, to mention but a few) and representing Present Day British English from the late 20th century.[4] As noun ellipsis with adjectives was anticipated to be marginal at best, a larger corpus was expected to yield more fruitful results. A further important requirement was the texts to be tagged for parts of speech, because the search was meant to cover the underlying construction and not particular lexemes.

The *Corpus of Contemporary American English* (COCA)[5] also meets the above requirements. Currently comprising 425 million words, it is even

4   *The Elliptical Noun Phrase in English*

more extensive than the BNC. However, as will be explained in Chapter 5, a search for elliptical noun phrases renders a great amount of data that needs manual analysis—a time-consuming procedure that would properly have been even more intricate with a larger corpus as the basis. This is the reason why the BNC was chosen for the main analysis, and the COCA is only used to retrieve examples that are not attested in the BNC.

It should be pointed out that variety-related issues had no share in this decision. This is because, as will be pointed out in the subsequent chapters, the morphosyntactic conditions on the use of nounless noun phrases are determined by the language's inflectional system. English, having an impoverished inflectional system, has rather strict conditions on the use of noun phrases without nouns, whereas a language with a richer inflectional system, such as German, allows more readily for the noun to be silent. Because British and American English do not differ with respect to inflectional morphology within the nominal domain, no differences in the licensing process are expected. The use of elliptical noun phrases will also be argued to be related to the coding of accessibility, which, according to Ariel (1990), is a cognitive category with a universal character. Thus, the occurrence of variety-specific differences is highly unlikely.

As has been pointed out, reference will be made to German. The German data used throughout this work stems from the Deutsche Referenzkorpus (German reference corpus), a collection of written language corpora that comprise 4.3 billion words of contemporary German from fictional, academic, and nonacademic prose.[6] The corpora are listed in the references.

1.3 THEORETICAL BACKGROUND AND TERMINOLOGY

This work attempts to provide an account of noun ellipsis that does away with the empirical issues of previous approaches, which will be outlined in Chapter 3. The aim is not to provide a technical implementation that is highly framework-bound; rather, the focus will be on drawing generalizations from the data that are independent of particular theoretical perspectives. The analysis presented in Chapter 4, for example, is compatible with both a traditional X-bar syntax approach where noun phrase is the topmost projection, dominating an N-bar and an N-level (see Jackendoff 1977), as well as with more recent approaches that consider the determiner the head of the structure (see Abney 1987). Similarly, it could be applied to an understanding of the nominal domain as a linear, that is, nonhierarchical, structure. This will become clear in the development of the analysis in Chapter 4.

I am well-aware, however, that certain assumptions have to be made and that they might be subject to discussion. The first of these is the existence of empty nominal elements. As mentioned in the previous section, it is assumed that noun phrases that lack a lexical noun contain an empty noun.

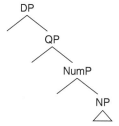

Figure 1.1 Syntactic representation of the nominal domain.

The latter can be overt (*one*-insertion) or silent (noun ellipsis). Furthermore, the noun phrase is considered to have a binary-branching, hierarchical structure (see Alexiadou et al. 2007 and references therein). Still, linear order is taken to have a considerable impact on the form, as will become clear in Chapter 4.

As the literature on noun ellipsis stems predominantly from what can be loosely subsumed under the term generative perspective, at this point a very brief outline of the general architecture of the noun phrase within this framework is in order. The nominal domain is structured as follows: the lexical projection NP is dominated by a number of functional projections, such as the determiner phrase (DP) and a quantifier phrase (QP). Furthermore, I assume that number is hosted in a separate functional projection NumP (see Ritter 1991), which is only available for noun phrases that denote countable entities (corresponding to Borer's 2005 classifier projection). The structure of the nominal domain is represented in Figure 1.1.

The term noun phrase as used in this work refers to the entire nominal expression, that is, to what is abbreviated DP. When I refer to components of the noun phrase, I use the corresponding abbreviations (e.g., NumP and QP).

In subsequent chapters, references will be made to several different prenominal elements, which will be subsumed under two main terms—adjectives and determiners. Even though Huddleston and Pullum's (2002) classification of some items as determiners might be controversial (*many*, for example, being compatible with the definite article, could also be considered an adjective), their system of determiners is adopted here because the data serving as a point of departure (see Chapter 2) also stem from Huddleston and Pullum's classification. This classification is unproblematic because, as will be argued in Chapter 4, the position and the syntactic nature of a prenominal element are not crucial for the licensing of noun ellipsis.

A list of all determiners is presented in example (7), which is based on Payne and Huddleston (2002: 256). Please note that the authors distinguish between "determiner" as word class and "determinative" as function—to simplify matters, this distinction is not drawn here.

6   *The Elliptical Noun Phrase in English*

(7) *the, a*   articles

    this, that, these, those   demonstrative determiners

    all, both   universal determiners

    each, every   distributive determiners

    some, any   existential determiners

    one, two, three, . . .   cardinal numerals

    either, neither   disjunctive determiners

    no, none   negative determiners

    another   alternative-additive determiner

    a few, a little, several, . . .   positive paucal determiners

    many, much, few, little, . . .   degree determiners

    enough, sufficient   sufficiency determiners

    which, what   interrogative determiners

Another category to be added is genitives. The phrasal genitive (a noun phrase with a genitival suffix) and a dependent genitive element, such as *my, your,* etc., can function as determiners as well.

With respect to adjectives, two main categories will be distinguished in this work: those that denote properties (descriptive adjectives) and those that do not. The latter are labeled discourse-referential adjectives, following Rijkhoff (2008), because they signal the status that a referent has within the discourse. In example (8), for instance, the discourse-referential modifier *same* tells the hearer to locate a particular referent, and the modifier *other* instructs them to identify the second member of a previously established set.

(8) I gave her the same/the other book. (Rijkhoff 2008: 798)

Some further clarification is needed with respect to the ellipsis site. For reasons outlined in Chapter 3 and Chapter 4, an approach is adopted that regards the noun phrases under consideration as containing an empty nominal element. This element is a noun devoid of descriptive contents, that is, it is semantically empty. This actually applies to two forms that have been mentioned so far: *one* and the ellipsis site, that is, the gap in nounless noun phrases. As Panagiotidis (2002, 2003a, b) argues, both elements are empty nouns, one being silent, the other being overt, because they do not contribute lexical meaning on their own (for a lengthy discussion see Section 3.1). This idea is adopted in this work.

Introduction 7

Chapter 2 of this book describes which elements license noun ellipsis in English, in which cases *one* is required, and which elements allow for neither of the two forms. Special attention is paid to the status of descriptive adjectives, because their ability to occur as modifiers of silent nouns is left somewhat unclear in the literature. In addition, the core facts about noun ellipsis in German are outlined in order to highlight language-specific differences. The data presented in Chapter 2 give rise to a couple of questions to be dealt with in the subsequent three chapters. They can be summarized as follows:

1. **Licensing conditions.** Which crucial properties must an element be endowed with in order to function as licensor of noun ellipsis? How far does this relate to structural properties of the nominal domain?
2. **The structure of the elliptical noun phrase.** What is the nature of the ellipsis site? What is the nature of *one*? How far are the two elements related?
3. **Language-specific differences.** Why is noun ellipsis in English subject to stricter requirements than in languages such as German? Which conditions hold for noun ellipsis in German?
4. **Adjectival modifiers.** Is English noun ellipsis licit with adjectival modifiers? And, should this actually be the case, which factors play a pivotal role in relaxing the rather strict requirement of *one*-insertion?

Before an analysis is developed, Chapter 3 discusses to what extent previous approaches have been apt to answer these questions. It will become clear that previous accounts display some empirical as well as theoretical deficiencies, especially when it to comes to the parallels between *one*-insertion and noun ellipsis (which are outlined at the beginning of Chapter 3), and noun ellipsis with adjectival modifiers.

In Chapter 4, an alternative analysis is presented. It does away with the issues outlined in Chapter 3, as it takes the parallels between noun ellipsis and *one*-insertion into consideration and identifies the choice between the two elements as variation on the surface, relating the phenomenon to the mass-count distinction in English. In a next step, the analysis is extended to noun ellipsis in German, where gender is argued to play a pivotal role.

Chapter 5 sets out to rectify the unclear data situation in terms of descriptive adjectives as modifiers in elliptical noun phrases. One major corpus study and two subsequent ones show that adjectival modifiers allow for noun ellipsis in English and that the phenomenon is even less marginal than expected. It is demonstrated that noun ellipsis with adjectives is determined by a number of factors, rather than being a uniform phenomenon.

Chapter 6 summarizes the previous chapters.

2 Licensors of Empty Nouns in English—Setting the Scene

The aim of this chapter is twofold: It outlines the empirical facts about noun ellipsis and presents the questions that will be dealt with in this study. The first part, Section 2.1, provides a detailed description of the elements that license noun ellipsis as well as *one*-insertion in order to provide an overview of the licensors, that is, elements that allow for the two nominal forms. As pointed out in Chapter 1, the data presented here are taken from Payne and Huddleston (2002), who render a detailed description of the elements that allow for the silent empty noun, as well as from Stirling and Huddleston (2002), who describe the use of *one*-insertion. The subsequent section shows that while it is generally agreed which determiners license noun ellipsis, matters become more controversial when it comes to adjectival modifiers. As will become evident in Section 2.1.3, the question that naturally arises is whether it is a particular type of adjective (e.g., a semantic class such as color) that licenses ellipsis of the nominal element and, should this be the case, what the crucial semantic and syntactic properties of this class are. However, before the questions are laid out in detail in Section 2.3, Section 2.2 renders a brief description of the phenomenon in German in order to provide a reference point for the conditions on noun ellipsis in English.

2.1 LICENSORS OF NOUN ELLIPSIS IN ENGLISH

2.1.1 Overview of Prenominal Items and the Heads They Take

Prenominal items in English can be classified according to the type of anaphoric nominal head they take: Some elements allow for an empty slot, that is, noun ellipsis only, while others only allow for *one*(s). A range of items allows for both forms and some are incompatible with nonlexical nominal material altogether. The latter comprise the singular indefinite article, dependent possessive determiners, and the dependent negative determiner *no*. However, all of these forms have counterparts that occur without nominal head, such as *none, mine, yours,* and the like. The indefinite article finds its counterpart in the numeral *one*. This stressed version of the indefinite article (Perlmutter 1970) can be used without lexical head.

Licensors of Empty Nouns in English—Setting the Scene 9

Table 2.1 Prenominal elements and anaphoric nominal forms

Noun ellipsis	Noun ellipsis and *one*-insertion	*One*-insertion
• *These, those*	• *Either, neither*	• *The* (+ post-modifier)
• *All, both*	• *Each*	• *Every*
• *Any, some*	• *Another, other*	• Descriptive adjectives(?)
• *Enough, sufficient*	• Discourse-referential adjectives: *same, next, last, following, previous,* ordinal numerals	• Singular demonstratives(?)
• *Several, a few, a little*		
• *Many, much, few, little*		
• *None*	• *Which*	
• Cardinal numerals	• Superlatives	
• Possessives (phrasal and independent)		

Table 2.1 gives an overview of the different prenominal elements and the nonlexical heads they take. The status of the question marks with descriptive adjectives and singular demonstratives will be clarified in the subsequent sections.

2.1.2 Determiners

Payne and Huddleston (2002: 412) point out that most determiners can occur in elliptical noun phrases. The following examples illustrate instances of elements that license noun ellipsis only, that is, where *one*-insertion is not possible. Those are plural demonstratives, cardinal numerals, as well as *both, any, some, several, many, more, most,* and possessives (phrasal genitives and independent possessive determiners, examples 1g and 1h) (Payne & Huddleston 2002: 373–416):

(1) a. Those cards are Kim's; **these** are yours.

    b. Her friends have got their results: **all/ both** have passed.

    c. I need some dollar coins; have you got **some** I could borrow?

    d. I wanted to buy some dollar coins but she didn't have **any.**

    e. This copy is defective but the other **two** are fine.

    f. I've corrected most of the mistakes but these **few** here are still to be done.

    g. Kim's car had broken down and **mine** had too.

    h. Alice's performance of the Schubert and **Helen's** of the Rachmaninov.

10   *The Elliptical Noun Phrase in English*

According to Stirling and Huddleston (2002: 1511ff), these elements cannot be used with nominal *one*. The same holds for cardinal numerals, *all, both, many, some, several, a few,* and *few,* as well as genitive constructions. But Stirling and Huddleston point out that in some nonstandard varieties of English, *one* is occasionally used with the genitive—*?She's finished her assignment, but I've only done half of my one* (ibid.: 1513).

Another type of determiner that is incompatible with *one*-insertion is a quantifier that quantifies over masses such as *much*.[1]

(2) I wanted some milk but there wasn't **much** (*one) left.

Discourse-referential adjectives, which do not denote properties but rather establish relations between referents, such as ordinal numerals, *next,* and *last,* as well as determiners such as *each, either, neither, which, another,* and *other* allow for both noun ellipsis and *one*-insertion (Payne & Huddleston 2002; Stirling & Huddleston 2002: 1511–1518). The following examples are taken from Stirling & Huddleston 2002).

(3) a. This bus is full: we'll have to wait for the **next** (one).

   b. The first student wanted to take linguistics, but the **second** (one) did not.

   c. These are excellent biscuits. Can I have **another** (one)?

   d. These seats are still available: **Which** (one(s)) do you want?

Both Payne and Huddleston and Stirling and Huddleston include singular demonstratives in the group of elements that occur in both kinds of constructions.

(4) a. This copy is clearer than **that** (one). (Stirling & Huddleston 2002: 1511)

   b. That sausage has only 25% percent meat, but **this** has 90%. (Payne & Huddleston 2002: 414)

However, it is pointed out that the construction in example (4b) "is somewhat less likely than one with pro-nominal *one*" (Payne & Huddleston 2002: 414). According to Lobeck (1995), Sleeman (2003), and Llombart-Huesca (2002), the singular demonstrative cannot license noun ellipsis. The nature of *this* and *that* and its interaction with silent nouns will be accounted for in Chapter 4, but suffice it to say at this point that these elements seem to be a more marginal licensor.

So far, restrictions have been outlined for *one*-insertion only. The following examples, taken from Payne and Huddleston (2002: 412f), show that neither a definite article nor the distributive determiner *every* appear in elliptical noun phrases:

(5) Alice's performance was better than the *(one) of Helen.

Licensors of Empty Nouns in English—Setting the Scene 11

(6) He received over a hundred letters and replied to **every** *(**one**).

Note that the indefinite singular article *a(n)* (in contrast to numeral *one*) neither allows for noun ellipsis nor *one*-insertion:

(7) I haven't got a pen, can you lend me **one**/ *a (**one**)? (ibid.: 412)

2.1.3 Adjectives

While discourse-referential modifiers allow for noun ellipsis, matters become more complex when it comes to descriptive adjectives in elliptical noun phrases. As Payne and Huddleston (2002: 416f) illustrate, the following adjectives are potential licensors of noun ellipsis: Superlatives and definite comparatives (example 8), "modifiers denoting colour, provenance and composition" (example 9), as well as adjectives that denote "basic physical properties such as age and size" (example 10).

(8) a. I went up that skyscraper in Boston, but **the tallest** is in Chicago.

   b. There are two sisters, but **the elder** is already married.

   c. *Hugo has a big house, but Karl has **a bigger**.
    (Payne & Huddleston 2002: 416)

(9) a. Henrietta likes red shirts, and I like **blue**.

   b. Knut wanted the French caterers, but I wanted **the Italian**.

   c. I prefer cotton shirts to **nylon**.
    (ibid.: 417)

(10) a. Lucie likes young dogs, but I prefer **old**.

   b. Lucie likes big dogs, but I prefer **small**.
    (ibid.)

Adjectives other than those denoting character and basic properties do not yield acceptable results:

(11) *Lucie likes friendly dogs, but I prefer **aggressive**. (ibid.)

As already indicated by example (8c), definiteness is another factor that plays a crucial role in terms of the construction's acceptability. According to Payne and Huddleston, the use of the indefinite article with the above adjectives either reduces the acceptability or it results in an unacceptable structure, as shown in the next two examples:

(12) ?Harvey bought a red shirt and I bought **a blue**.

12 *The Elliptical Noun Phrase in English*

(13) *Lucie bought a young dog, but I bought **an old.**
     (ibid.: 417)

The above data suggest that the licensing of noun ellipsis is tied to certain semantic classes of adjectives, but matters are not as straightforward as they may seem. Not only is there considerable disagreement in the literature as to which adjectives allow for the noun to remain silent in English, some approaches even deny the existence of the phenomenon altogether. Sleeman (1996: 50ff), for example, claims that in English, color adjectives are the only descriptive adjectives that allow for the noun (or the nominal) to be omitted (see also Lobeck 1995: 67n5; but see Lobeck 2006), whereas, for example, Llombart-Huesca (2002) marks examples as the one outlined in example (9a) as ungrammatical (*I like the blue car but I don't like the pink* [Llombart-Huesca 2002: 66]) and claims that *one* has to be inserted to get an acceptable structure. Bouchard (2002) also claims that noun ellipsis with modifying adjectives is generally absent in English, but he states that it is possible in a very salient context, that is, when a sharp contrast is expressed, the content of the nominal can be recovered (ibid.: 226). He presents the following oft-quoted examples by Halliday and Hasan (1976; in Bouchard 2002: 225; see also Sleeman 1996: 51n18).

(14) I like strong tea. I suppose weak is better for you.[2]

(15) Which last longer, the curved rods or the straight rods? The straight are less likely to break.

Panagiotidis (2003a) also attributes the choice between noun ellipsis (what he considers to be an empty noun) and *one*-insertion to extra-linguistic, that is, pragmatic aspects, when he states "they [*one* and noun ellipsis] should be in free variation and indeed, if the pragmatic context is right, they are, even in a language like English" (ibid.: 423).

2.2 Noun Ellipsis in German

The differences between the German and the English noun phrase relevant for the present analysis pertain to inflectional properties. In the German noun phrase, gender (masculine, feminine, neuter), number (singular and plural), and case (nominative, genitive, dative, accusative) are morphologically encoded.[3] Gender is a category inherent to nouns, whereas adjectives and determiners agree with the gender of the head noun, that is, their morphological form is determined by the category of the nominal head. Case is determined by the syntactic role of the noun phrase, and number is selected according to its reference.

Another aspect that is important for the present analysis is the traditional distinction of different types of adjectival morphology—strong inflection

Licensors of Empty Nouns in English—Setting the Scene 13

and weak inflection.[4] The choice of the type is dependent on the determiner preceding the adjective. Uninflected determiners and the zero determiner are followed by a strongly inflected adjective, as in example (16a); the definite article, demonstratives, and quantifying determiners except for *kein* (no) take a weakly inflected adjective, as illustrated in example (16b).

(16) a. manch arm-**es** Mädchen
some poor.NOM.NEUT.SG girl

   b. das arm-e Mädchen
DEF poor.NOM.NEUT.SG girl

With respect to noun ellipsis in German, there are two important aspects. First, there is no strategy comparable to *one*-insertion; second, noun ellipsis seems much less constrained than in English. The following examples demonstrate that descriptive adjectives, examples (17–18), as well as discourse-referential ones, examples (19–20). occur in elliptical noun phrases:

(17) Abbott   bemühte sich 1608, eine Vereinigung der schottischen
Abbott   tried   REFL 1608 a   union   the Scottish
<u>Episkopalkirche</u>   mit der   **englischen**
Episcopal
Church.GEN.FEM.SG   with the   English.DAT.FEM.SG
zustande zu bringen.
bring about

"In 1608 Abbot tried to unite the Scottish Episcopal Church and the English (Episcopal Church)."
(WPD/AAA.00420)

(18) An   den öffentlichen <u>Teil</u>   schließt sich   noch ein
to   the public   part.ACC.MASC.SG follows REFL also a
nichtöffentlicher   an.
non-public.NOM.MASC.SG on

"The public part is followed by a non-public one."
(RHZ07/JAN.12314)

(19) Aber sicherlich ist   diese   <u>Etappe</u>   nicht die **letzte**   auf
but definitely is   this   stage.NOM.FEM.SG not   the last.NOM.FEM.SG on
dem Weg   zur   Vereinigung Europas.
the way   to the union   Europe

"But definitively this stage won't be the last one on the way to a united Europe."
(B05/MAI.41473)

14 *The Elliptical Noun Phrase in English*

(20) Ein <u>Opfer</u> starb, ein **zweites** wurde
one victim.NOM.NEUT.SG died, a second.NOM.NEUT.SG was
verletzt geborgen.
injured rescued

"One victim died, a second (one) was rescued injured."
(DPA09/FEB.06799)

The modifiers have the same form as when used attributively with an overt noun, that is, lexical nouns could be inserted into the structure (*der englischen Episkopalkirche, einnichtöffentlicher Teil, die letzte Etappe, ein zweites Opfer*). The examples also indicate that elliptical noun phrases can be definite and indefinite, that is, there is no definiteness requirement. Furthermore, both weak and strong inflectional endings are licit.

Determiners such as demonstratives (example 21), quantifiers (example 22), the definite article (example 23), and distributive determiners (example 24) also allow for noun ellipsis, as evident in the following examples:

(21) . . . private <u>Projekte</u> wie **jenes** in der Kreisstadt
private projects.NOM.NEUT.PL like that.NOM.NEUT.SG in the county seat

". . . private projects like the one in the county seat"
(RHZ06/DEZ.28658)

(22) Von solchen <u>Konferenzen</u> gibt es in der Erzählung
of such conferences.DAT.FEM.PL exist EXPL in the narrative
mehrere.
several.DAT.PL

"There are several of those conferences in the narrative."
(HAZ08/JAN.01127)

(23) Wir sehen unseren <u>Horizont</u> weiter als **den**
we consider our ken.ACC.MASC.SG broader than the.ACC.MASC.SG
der Kirchen.
the church

"We consider our ken to be broader than the one of the churches."
(RHZ09/NOV.13631)

(24) Ich werde das <u>Spiel</u> angehen wie jedes **andere**
I will the game.ACC.NEUT.SG approach like every other ACC.NEUT.SG
auch.
too

"I will approach this game like any other."
(HAZ07/NOV.02830)

Licensors of Empty Nouns in English—Setting the Scene 15

Table 2.2 Inflection of *ein, kein, mein*

| | Singular | | | Plural |
	Masc.	Fem.	Neut.	
Nominative	—	*-e*	—	*-e*
Genitive	*-es*	*-er*	*-es*	*-er*
Dative	*-em*	*-er*	*-em*	*-en*
Accusative	*-en*	*-e*	—	*-e*

Even though it may seem as if there are no morphosyntactic constraints on noun ellipsis in German, this is not entirely true. Items with a defective inflectional paradigm such as the indefinite article, possessive determiners, and *kein* "no" (labeled "*ein*-words" by Lobeck 1995) do not readily allow for noun ellipsis. This affects only some forms of the paradigm outlined in Table 2.2 (see Zifonun et al. 1997: 1933; Eisenberg 2006: 176), namely the uninflected ones that call for strong inflectional endings on the adjective—nominative masculine and neuter singular, as well as accusative neuter singular.

The inflected versions readily occur in elliptical noun phrases, as shown in example (25), where the corresponding head noun *Fahrkarte* "ticket" has feminine gender:

(25) Als sie seine   <u>Fahrkarte</u>   sehen wollte, musste er zugeben,
     when she his   ticket.ACC.FEM.SG see wanted must he admit

     dass er **keine**   hatte
     that he no. ACC.FEM.SG had

     "When she wanted to see his ticket, he had to admit that he had none."
     (NUN09/NOV.00438)

However, the uninflected versions cannot be used elliptically. In cases of ellipsis, a form is employed that is restricted to the use without a nominal element. This is evident in example (26), where the antecedent *Bild* "picture" is neuter: with an overt noun, *kein* remains uninflected; without a noun, *kein* is inflected (provided it is nominative).

(26) Aber   in der Garderobe   war kein <u>Bild</u>   von ihrem
     but   in the checkroom   was no   picture.NOM.NEUT.SG of   her

     Mann   und auch **keines**   von dem Kind.
     husband and also no.NOM.NEUT.SG of   the   child

     "But in the checkroom there was no picture of her husband and none of the child either."
     (HMP09/MAR.00847)

16 *The Elliptical Noun Phrase in English*

The following data show that no difference with dative case is evident—the negative determiner has the same inflectional endings as in attributive position.

(27) a.

Das	beweisen	schon	ihre	Bilder.	Auf
that	prove	already	their	pictures.NOM.NEUT.PL	on
keinem	ist	der	Unfall	zu	sehen.
no.DAT.NEUT.SG	is	the	accident	to	see

"That is already proven by their pictures. In none the accident is shown."
(HAZ07/OKT.01740)

b.

Auf	**keinem**	**Bild**	von	Karol Rousin
on	no.DAT.NEUT.SG	picture.DAT.NEUT.SG	of	Karol Rousin

"in no picture by Karol Rousin"
(RHZ07/JAN.27471)

A similar situation obtains with adjectives—they have to be inflected, too. Because adjectives in attributive position usually inflect in German, this may not be too evident. However, there is a range of adjectives that cannot inflect. They comprise some adjectives of value such as *prima* "super," *klasse* "excellent," and *super* "super, some color-denoting ones such as *lila* "purple" or *rosa* "pink," as well as some loan words from English such as *sexy* or *trendy* (see Duden 2009: 344f). These noninflecting adjectives do not allow for noun ellipsis:

(28)

Anna	trägt	eine blaue	Mütze,	nicht eine	*rosa.
Anna	wears	a blue	hat.ACC.FEM.SG	not a	pink

"Anna is wearing a blue hat, not a pink one."
(ibid.: 341)

Interestingly, the inflecting (nonstandard) counterparts that exist for some of these adjectives occur in elliptical noun phrases, as pointed out by Sleeman (1996). For the color adjectives *lila* and *rosa,* for example, there are two ways to obtain inflected versions: the nonstandard *lilane* or *rosane,* and compounds such as *lila-/rosa-farben* or *lila-/rosafarbig* "purple-/pink-colored." These inflected items occur without nominal head:

(29)

An	einem	besonderen	Tag	wie	an	Weihnachten	oder	Ostern	trägt	man
on	a	special	day	like	on	Christmas	or	Easter	wears	one
als	Pfarrer	ein	weißes	Messgewand,	an	normalen				
as	priest	a	white	liturgical garment.ACC. NEUT.SG	on	ordinary				

Tagen	ein	**grünes,**	in	der	Fastenzeit	ein	**lilanes,**
days	a	green.ACC. NEUT.SG	in	the	lent	a	purple. ACC.NEUT. SG

am	Karfreitag	ein	**rotes.**
on the	Good Friday	a	red.ACC. NEUT.SG

"On a special day such as Christmas or Easter priests wear a white liturgical garment, on ordinary days a green one, during lent a purple one and on Good Friday a red one."
(M07/APR.02637)

Licensors of Empty Nouns in English—Setting the Scene 17

(30)

Der	rote	<u>Umschlag</u>		muss	in	den	**lilafarbenen**
The	red	envelope.NOM.MASC.SG		must	in	the	purple-colored.ACC.MASC.SG
gesteckt	werden.						
put	be.						

"The red envelope has to be put into the purple one."
(Z07/FEB.00438)

(31)

Die	knallbunten	<u>Stücke</u>	daneben	wurden	in	Amerika
the	brightly-colored	items.NOM.NEUT.PL	alongside	were	in	America
bestellt,	die	weichen	**rosafarbigen**	etwa,	die	den	Arm
ordered	the	soft	rose-colored. NOM. PL	for example REL	the	arm
fast	zur	Gänze	bedecken,	gehen	nach	Los Angeles.
almost	to the	entirety	cover	go	to	Los Angeles

"The brightly colored items next to it were ordered in America, the soft rose ones for example,
which cover almost the entire arm, will be shipped to Los Angeles."
(B07/OKT.74374)

To sum up, in German, the element preceding the ellipsis site has to be inflected. Because most prenominal elements inflect, noun ellipsis in German appears to be less constrained than noun ellipsis in English. The sole exception to this is the plural cardinal numeral—even though it has lost most of its inflectional properties, it licenses noun ellipsis. The inflectional endings that were retained include the following: a strong genitive form -er for *zwei* "two" and *drei* "three," and a dative form -en for *zwei* "two" to *zwölf* "twelve" without *sieben* "seven," that is used if no element bearing the same case, that is, no noun, follows (Duden 2009: 383f), as in example (32).

(32)

Erst	ein	<u>Spiel</u>	von	**dreien**	haben	sie	gewonnen . . .
only	one	match.ACC.NEUT.SG	of	three.DAT. PL	have	they	won

"They have won only one match out of three . . ."
(SOZ08/DEZ.01605)

However, a noninflected dative form is attested in elliptical uses as well:

(33)

Die	französischen	Ambulanzen	sind	grundsätzlich	mit	einem
the	French	ambulances	are	generally	with	a
<u>Notarzt</u>	ausgestattet,	manchmal	sogar	mit		
emergency physician.DAT.MASC.SG	equipped	sometimes	even	wit		
zwei	–im	Unterschied	zu	den	USA, . . .	
two	in the	contrast	to	the	USA	

"There is generally an emergency physician on board French ambulances, sometimes
there are even two—in contrast to the USA, . . ."
(B98/FEB.08686)

18 *The Elliptical Noun Phrase in English*

(34) . . . vier   Tickets   zum   Preis   von   **drei** . . .
four   ticket.ACC.PL   for the   price   of   three

"four tickets for the price of three"
(B03/DEZ.85443)

It is also noteworthy that in some cases numerals in elliptical noun phrases display the suffix *-e*. According to Duden (2009), this form can be found in "older" literature, such as in the following example from Thomas Mann, and in some nonstandard varieties.

(35) . . .   von den   englischen Schriftstellern,   auf die Sie hinweisen,
of   the   English   writer.DAT.MASC.PL on REL you refer

kenne ich **zweie** recht   gut.
know I   two-e   quite   well

"Of the English writers you are referring to I know two quite well."
(THM/AM3.06888)

The final important aspect to be pointed out here relates to the position of the inflected element in the prenominal string. In elliptical noun phrases, only the item immediately preceding the ellipsis site has to be inflected. This is illustrated in the following examples:

(36) Das   ist auch eine Art   Spiel,   aber kein
That   is also a   kind game. NOM.NEUT.SG but no

schönes.
nice.NOM.NEUT.SG

"That is also a kind of game, but not a nice one."
(BRZ09/DEZ.00446)

(37) Welches   Schulfach   ist   dein   **liebstes?**
Which   subject.NOM.NEUT.SG   is   your   favorite.NOM.NEUT.SG

"Which subject is your favorite?"
(BRZ09/FEB.11066)

(38) Mein Auto   ist   Jahrgang   1985, und für **ein neues**
my   car.NOM.NEUT.SG is   year   1985 and for a   new.DAT.NEUT.SG

ist   kein   Geld   vorhanden.
is   no   money present

"My car is from 1985 and there is no money for a new one."
(B97/OKT.00690)

Licensors of Empty Nouns in English—Setting the Scene 19

In these elliptical noun phrases, *ein*-words are not inflected, although the phrases under consideration bear accusative case and have neuter antecedents. Similarly, adjectives can remain uninflected as long as the last one in the prenominal adjective string (a present participle in the next example) bears inflectional endings:

(39)

Neben	den	von	Andreina in Ertico		Wolfsburg erstandenen
In addition	the	from	Andreina in Ertico		Wolfsburg purchased
<u>Siegerschuhen</u>	gefielen	Linna Hensel	ganz	besonders	
winner shoe.DAT.MASC.PL	liked	Linna Hensel	very	especially	
auffallend	grün-farbene, moderne		schwarze	und	**sexy**	lila
strikingly	green-colored modern		black	and	sexy	purple
glitzernde.					
glitter.PART.NOM.PL					

"Apart from the winner's shoes Andreina Ertico bought in Wolfsburg, Linna Hensel especially like strikingly green ones, modern black ones and sexy purple glittering ones." (BRZ08/MAI.16014)

In this context, *sexy* is licit, even though it remains uninflected.

2.3 Questions to Be Addressed

The above sections give rise to a number of questions relating to the licensing of noun ellipsis. The first one, to be addressed in Chapter 4, concerns the properties the licensors must have, that is, the question whether any generalizations in terms of common features can be drawn from Table 2.1. Very closely connected is the issue of the nature of *one*—how far are elliptical noun phrases and those containing *one* related? What role does *one* play in the noun phrase? A follow-up question pertains to typological aspects—why are there stricter requirements for English than for a language such as German? Does this derive from general language-specific properties such as the inventory of inflectional markings available within the noun phrase, as has been claimed, for example, by Lobeck (1995)?

The second aspect to be dealt with in this chapter relates to the structure of the elliptical noun phrase, in particular to the nature of what has been called the ellipsis site in this work. There are several options. First, the ellipsis site could contain a structurally available but phonetically deleted representation of the antecedent (which would qualify the phenomenon under examination as "true" ellipsis), a process to be called PF-deletion, following Merchant (2001), among others. Second, the ellipsis site could be "filled" by an empty nominal element, either the pronominal form *pro* (see, e.g., Lobeck 1995; Kester 1996; Sleeman 1996) or an empty noun (Panagiotidis

20 *The Elliptical Noun Phrase in English*

2003a, b). Third, the element preceding the ellipsis site or, in other words, the rightmost element in the (formerly) prenominal string, could have taken over the position of the nominal head (see, e.g., Halliday & Hasan 1976). Fourth, this element could have a dual function of determiner/modifier and head, a fusion of prenominal material and head, as proposed by Payne and Huddleston (2002).

The unclear data situation outlined above gives rise to further questions (to be dealt with on the basis of a corpus analysis in Chapter 5). The first and obvious one is whether noun ellipsis with adjectival modifiers is licit in English. Should this be the case, the analysis has to show whether is it a particular type of adjective that occurs in this construction (Payne & Huddleston 2002) or rather a particular context that allows for the use of adjectives without head nouns (see, e.g., Bouchard 2002). If the former scenario turns out to be the correct one, the semantico-pragmatic features of the adjectives and their syntactic positions[5] require closer scrutiny. If, on the other hand, the latter scenario applies, a thorough analysis of contextual factors, such as the syntactic context and the discourse situation, is needed in order to put forth any generalizations. In both cases, the findings have to be integrated into the analysis presented in Chapter 4 in order to provide a full picture of noun ellipsis in English.

A final question to be addressed is in how far the analysis to be proposed for noun ellipsis can be extended to capture the other types of nounless noun phrases outlined in Chapter 1.

3 Inflection, Focus, and Partitivity— Previous Accounts of Noun Ellipsis

This chapter provides a discussion of previous approaches to noun ellipsis with respect to the questions outlined in Chapter 2. These approaches can roughly be divided into (a) those that consider inflection or morphosyntactic properties of a licensor to be the crucial features, (b) those that relate the licensing to semantic features, and (c) those that take noun phrase-internal properties such as topic and contrastive focus into account.

Section 3.1 starts out with a more detailed description of the properties of elliptical noun phrases and those containing *one*, respectively, in order to provide a point of departure to discuss the empirical accuracy of the various approaches. Section 3.2 presents two inflectional approaches (Lobeck 1995; Kester 1996b). Section 3.3 discusses the semantic notion of partitivity introduced by (Sleeman 1996), which has been highly influential (see, e.g., Bouchard 2002; Gengel 2007; Valois & Royle 2009; Alexiadou & Gengel forthcoming). The first subsection is devoted to Sleeman's account, the second to general issues of the notion of partitivity. In Section 3.4 information structural accounts (Corver & van Koppen 2009 [Section 3.4.1]; Eguren 2010 [Section 3.4.2]) are given consideration. Section 3.5 outlines the idea that *one* is a classifier-like element, put forth by Alexiadou and Gengel (forthcoming) and Llombart-Huesca (2002). Section 3.6 summarizes the chapter.

3.1 TWO EMPTY NOUNS AND THEIR PROPERTIES

In order to discuss the merits and weaknesses of previous approaches to noun ellipsis in English, a closer look at the properties of nounless noun phrases is indispensable. In the previous chapter, it was shown that prenominal elements either allow for *one*, for noun ellipsis, or for both.[1] The question that arises at this point is in which other respects noun ellipsis and *one*-insertion differ crucially or whether they converge in some respect. As mentioned in Chapter 1, *one* and noun ellipsis are considered to involve (semantically) empty nouns—*one* being overt, the other being silent, following Panagiotidis (2003a, b). In what follows, a detailed comparison of the two forms is provided to support this assumption.

22 *The Elliptical Noun Phrase in English*

First of all, there are distributional properties that *one* and noun ellipsis share (outlined by Llombart-Huesca 2002: 62–65; the following examples are hers).[2] These include the ability of the anaphoric relation to cross-utterance boundaries (example 1), and that there is no required linguistic realization of the antecedent (examples 2–3).

(1) Which car do you like?
    a. I like **these.**
    b. I like **the pink one.**

(2) (looking at some cars): Do you like **those?**

(3) (at a car dealer's): **Which one** do you like?
    I like the pink one.

Furthermore, both noun ellipsis and *one* cannot take complements (example 4), whereas they can take postnominal modifiers (example 5).[3]

(4) a. *I talked with <u>these students of physics</u> and with **these of chemistry.**
    b. *<u>The destruction of Rome</u> was as cruel as **the one of Carthage.**

(5) a. I talked with <u>these students from Germany</u> and with **these from Italy.**
    b. I met <u>the student from Germany</u> but I didn't meet **the one from Italy.**

As pointed out, for example, by Keizer (2011: 320), *one* can substitute for more than just the head noun. This becomes clear in cases where the antecedent noun is modified by more than one adjective, as in the following example:

(6) John likes that <u>big black French car.</u>
    a. Jane likes **the small red one.**
    b. Jane likes **the small one.**
    c. Jane likes **this one.**
    (ibid.)

For elliptical noun phrases, it is somewhat more difficult to make a parallel visible, because adjectival modifiers are (usually, see Chapter 2) followed by *one*. Nevertheless, there are data that suggest that noun ellipsis can also target more than just the nominal head. In the following two examples,

Inflection, Focus, and Partitivity—Previous Accounts of Noun Ellipsis 23

the elliptical noun phrase can be understood to include the modifier of the antecedent:

(7) What do you think of the tone of <u>these inaugural festivities</u> compared to **those you've seen in the past?** (COCA, 2001, SPOK)

(8) . . . a pattern that linked <u>these semi-detached houses</u> of Wanley with **those** in Leeds and Northam (BNC, FB0)

The addressee in example (7) has probably witnessed *inaugural* festivities before; similarly, in example (8) semi-detached houses of Wanley are connected to *semi-detached* houses in Leeds and Northam. This contrasts with the following examples, where the context makes an interpretation that includes the modifier of the antecedent unlikely.

(9) . . . the stage is ostensibly set for the viewer to compare <u>these peculiar juxtapositions</u> with **those more commonly seen in the media** . . . (BNC, HAD)

(10) <u>These private questions</u> are much like **those in our political conversations today.** (COCA, 2007, ACAD)

In example (9), peculiar juxtapositions are contrasted with common ones—contrast is expressed in a postmodifying clause rather than in the prenominal string. In the same vein, in example (10), private questions are compared with questions in political debates, that is, with questions that are discussed in public.

Apart from their distributional properties, elliptical noun phrases and those containing *one* display considerable overlap with respect to semantic properties. This is due to both forms being devoid of lexical meaning—both are anaphoric and hence need an antecedent in order to be interpretable, even though the latter does not necessarily have to be linguistically realized. The type of anaphora encoded in the present cases is a rather special one, because neither of the two forms substitutes for the full noun phrase (as pronouns do). Rather, the anaphoric relation holds below phrase level. This implies that in terms of *one*-insertion and noun ellipsis, the phrase containing the antecedent is not coreferential with the phrase containing the anaphoric form, as is the case for pronominal noun phrases. The following examples illustrate this difference. In example (11), the two highlighted noun phrases refer to the same entity; in example (12) and example (13) they do not.

(11) <u>Mrs. Thatcher</u> has been such a figure and, in spite of reverses, **she** has animated and directed governments with a sense of political direction. (BNC, A6F)

24 The Elliptical Noun Phrase in English

(12) First, does the child know that <u>the red stick</u> is longer than **the yellow one?** (BNC, EF8)

(13) Butter the bread, spread peanut butter on <u>four slices</u> and mayonnaise on **the other four.** (BNC, B29)

The relations between the two phrases will be subject to more thorough examination in Chapter 4. Suffice it to underline at this point that the phenomenon presented here relates to what has been referred to as contrast condition (Giannakidou & Stavrou 1999) or non-identity condition (Eguren 2010) in the literature; the two (or more) noun phrases are not referentially identical. This semantic non-identity also affects the choice of the modifier; as the two noun phrases denote different entities, difference is likely to be expressed through modifiers in the phrase. In example (12), there are two different modifiers (*red* and *yellow*), and in example (13), the adjective *other* signals non-identity.

To put it differently, the head noun (or the nominal) that serves as antecedent denotes a class. The two (or more) noun phrases, that is, the one containing the antecedent and the one(s) containing the anaphoric form(s), denote different instantiations, or members, of that class. The property that distinguishes these different members is expressed with the help of modifiers, which thus are necessarily restrictive. This distinction can also be expressed along other dimensions, such as quantity when it comes to numerals, distance when it comes to demonstratives, and the like.

What is important for the present argument is that these conditions apply to both anaphoric forms. In other words, on the semantic level, *one* and noun ellipsis are subject to the same conditions.

Further parallels between both forms display in terms of a non–antecedent-based use. As mentioned in Chapter 1, there is a type of nounless noun phrase that gets a default interpretation as [+human] if no antecedent is available. An example is provided below.

(14) Daniel does not seem to expect a universal resurrection of **the dead.** (BNC, H0K)

Interestingly, *one* can be used without antecedent to obtain human reference as well:

(15) Last night, perhaps, the bombs that fell from Rob's plane had killed women and children and old, helpless men, but for all that he was a tender lover. She wished **the dead ones** could have known that. (BNC, CEH 489–90)

(16) Everyone on this flight seemed utterly expendable, even the partial person in first class, the " human organ " in the cooler box, on its way to **some poor one** strapped in a hospital bed. (COCA, 2001 FIC)

Inflection, Focus, and Partitivity—Previous Accounts of Noun Ellipsis 25

I will come back to this in Section 4.3.2.3.

In light of the above, it is evident that *one* and noun ellipsis are closely related—there are obvious parallels that suggest that the two forms are different manifestations of one underlying phenomenon. Both are devoid of lexical meaning, that is, they denote no semantic concept. Both are subject to the same semantic conditions (non-identity/contrast) and display the same distributional properties (modifiers but no complements). They differ with respect to their phonological form: *one* is overt and hosts number morphology. Further, as illustrated in Chapter 2, their distribution is determined by particular prenominal elements. This, however, will be argued to be just a superficial difference in Chapter 4: As soon as a silent noun combines with number morphology, it can surface as *one*, a descriptively empty count noun that is deleted if countability is expressed on an adjacent element. Therefore, the only difference between the two is *one* being overt and countable.

This implies that noun ellipsis is considered to involve an empty nominal element as well. For a detailed discussion of the nature of the ellipsis site, the reader is referred to Chapter 4. Suffice it to state for the present purpose that there are two versions of a descriptively empty noun, one being silent and the other being overt.

The observant reader may have noticed that the above data apparently contradict the claim that *one* and its silent counterpart are nouns, because they can substitute for more than just the head noun (see examples 6–8), and they cannot take complements (example 4). However, these problems are more apparent than real. As Schütze (2001) and Panagiotidis (2003b) (crediting Radford 1989) point out, the latter aspect derives from their lack of lexical meaning. Due to the fact that these nouns do not denote predicates, they do not have argument structure, that is, they cannot select complements (Schütze 2001: 134).[4] The fact that the forms seem to be hosted in N-bar rather than N (Jackendoff 1977) is not considered to be structurally determined, but that it takes place at the semantic level. Schütze supports this claim by drawing a parallel to the interpretation of pronouns: A personal pronoun such as *he*, for example, can take an antecedent such as the rather complex phrase *the man standing over there* and, according to Schütze, "no one would claim that in the syntax *he* actually contains all the internal structure that its antecedent has" (2001: 135).

3.2 INFLECTION AND AGREEMENT

Lobeck (1995), Kester (1996a, b), and Sleeman (1996) regard the empty noun as a base-generated empty pronoun *pro* that needs to be licensed and identified, as proposed by Rizzi (1986) for subject *pro* in pro-drop languages. Licensing refers to the syntactic process that makes an empty element licit; identification means that its features have to be identified or "made visible" in order for the form to be interpretable.[5]

26 *The Elliptical Noun Phrase in English*

3.2.1 Lobeck's Analysis

According to Lobeck (1995), the empty category, small *pro*, has to be licensed by an element specified for strong agreement: "[a]n empty, non-arbitrary pronominal must be properly head-governed, and governed by an X^0 specified for strong agreement" (ibid.: 41). Strong agreement is defined as follows:

> An X^0 is specified for strong agreement if X^0, or the phrase of the head with which X^0 agrees, morphologically realizes agreement in a productive number of cases. (Lobeck 1995: 51)

According to this definition, the agreement features can either be morphologically realized on the head that licenses *pro* or on the elements the head agrees with, that is, its complement or specifier. The features are located in Num or Det, the heads of functional projections dominating NP.[6] In English, for example, the most obvious strong agreement feature is [+plural] because it is morphologically realized on the noun and can be visible on the determiner (e.g., in the case of demonstratives) through agreement.

The number of features that are required for licensing the empty category correlates with the number of possible strong agreement features in the noun phrase system of a particular language. Lacking a rich inflectional system, English only has three relevant features: [+plural], [+possessive], and [+partitive]. The existence of the former two is evident; the latter, however, requires further elaboration.

In Lobeck's account, [+partitive] is defined as the ability to occur in a partitive construction. Elements such as numerals or the plural indefinite article, for example, can take a partitive prepositional phrase:

(17) a. **two** of the cars

　　　b. **some** of the cars

Interestingly, an element's ability to fill this slot in the partitive construction correlates with its ability to license noun ellipsis, as illustrated in example (18) (see Lobeck 1995: 93):

(18) a. The women came in and **each**/***every** sat down.

　　　b. **each** of the women

　　　c. ***every** of the women

As (18a) shows, *each* can license noun ellipsis, whereas *every* cannot (see also Chapter 2). Similarly, *each* can take a partitive prepositional phrase (PP), whereas *every* cannot. On the basis of this observation, Lobeck concludes that *each* is a partitive element, but *every* is not. The partitivity

Inflection, Focus, and Partitivity—Previous Accounts of Noun Ellipsis 27

feature on *each* licenses the empty pronominal. I will come back to this in Section 3.2.2.

The postulated plurality feature is more intuitive. The plural demonstratives *these* and *those*, for instance, are specified for [+plural]. According to Lobeck, this suffices to obtain strong agreement—plural is morphosyntactically realized in English. Quantifiers and numerals on the other hand are specified for strong agreement by a [+partitive] feature for singular and by [+partitive, +plural] for plural. Examples (19) and (20) exemplify the DP's representation in Lobeck's (1995) account:

(19) Mary likes those books but I like [$_{DP}$ **these** [$_{NumP}$ *e* [$_{NP}$ *e*]]].

(20) The students attended the play but [$_{NumP}$ **many/few/six** [$_{NP}$ *e*]] left disappointed.

German, in contrast, being a highly inflected language, needs determiners to be morphologically specified for two strong agreement features ([+gender], [+case]) and quantifiers to be specified for three features ([+gender], [+case], [+partitive]) in order to license the empty pronominal.

The relevant difference between English and German is that adjectives in German, unlike in English, show inflectional endings as well. They can be specified for strong agreement and, hence, can be used as modifiers in elliptical noun phrases, as indicated in Section 2.2.

French adjectives are subject to similar requirements; they must be specified for gender and number to license noun ellipsis. Thus, in example (21), where the adjectives *grand* "big" and *petit* "small" are endowed with gender and number features, the empty pronominal is licit:

(21) J'ai vu les garcons dans le cours. Les **grands** [*e*] jouaient avec les **petits** [*e*].

I saw the boys in the courtyard. The big ones were playing with the small ones. (Lobeck 1995: 131)

The absence of these features on English adjectives is considered to be the reason for the adjectives' inability license *pro* (see also Lobeck 2006). In other words, noun ellipsis with adjectives is not licit, due to the fact that adjectives are neither specified for partitivity nor for number (or plurality).

3.2.2 Kester's Analysis

Kester (1996a, 1996b) provides an approach similar to Lobeck's to account for noun ellipsis in Dutch. She also attributes the differences between noun ellipsis English and noun ellipsis in another Germanic language, Dutch, to the presence or absence of adjectival morphology. Dutch adjectives need an

28   *The Elliptical Noun Phrase in English*

inflectional suffix –*e*,[7] pronounced schwa, in order to modify a silent noun, as exemplified in example (22). This ending is only absent when the DP is specified for [+neuter, +singular, -definite], as shown in example (23):

(22)   de   rode   auto   en   de   **groene**   [e]
      the   red   car   and   the   green   (one)

(23) a.   de **grote** man, het **grote** huis
      "the tall man." "the big house"

   b.   een **grot** huis
      "a big house"
      (Kester 1996a: 68)

Interestingly, in the case of the latter, that is, with an adjective that does not bear an inflectional ending, noun ellipsis is often considered to be unacceptable. However, as Kester points out, some speakers use schwa, even though this inflectional ending is not required to agree with a lexical noun (see Section 3.4.1):

(24) a.   *een rod boek en een *groen* [e]
      a red book and a green

   b.   Jan   had   voor Marie   een rood boek gekocht, maar zij had
      John   had   for   Mary   a   red   book bought   but   she had
      veel   liever   een   *groene* [e].
      much rather a   green

      "John had bought a red book for Mary, but she preferred a green one."
      (ibid.: 69)

Schwa licenses *pro,* and the lexical antecedent identifies it. Kester (1996b) further specifies the licensing mechanism. She assumes a functional projection FP dominating NP whose specifier contains an AP. The -*e* suffix on the adjective makes the functional head F^0 visible, which, in turn, can license *pro.* Similarly, adjectival inflection in English superlative constructions can carry out this function. In terms of noninflected, that is, nongraded adjectives, *one*-insertion into F^0 is required to make the functional head visible; *one,* being an inflected element, enables F^0 to license *pro.* It is considered the counterpart of the adjectival morphology found in Dutch and German noun ellipsis contexts.

Kester further argues that *one* is an element specified for [+count]. This is because it is incompatible with mass readings (as has already been pointed out in footnote 2 in Chapter 2). She presents the following example from Quirk et al. (1982: 870):

(25) Shall I pass the butter? Or have you got *one/some already?

Inflection, Focus, and Partitivity—Previous Accounts of Noun Ellipsis 29

The countability specification of *one* makes its insertion following quantifiers redundant.

Numerals and quantifiers are considered to head FP, where they properly govern *pro*. Their [+count] features identify *pro*. An adjective blocks this licensing mechanism. Hence, *one* is needed to make the functional projection governing *pro* visible.

3.2.3 Against Formal Licensing and Identification

The approaches that relate noun ellipsis to inflectional properties can be maintained to some extent. I follow Lobeck in that nongraded descriptive adjectives do not license noun ellipsis in English because they are uninflected. The claim that plurality plays a crucial role in the licensing process is adopted in the present approach as well. However, as will be argued in Chapter 4, the absence of inflection on adjectives results in them being unspecified in terms of countability. Therefore, it is not the absence of inflectional morphology (or plural morphology) that blocks noun ellipsis but the absence of a crucial property—countability—that can be expressed through plural morphology (similar to what has been claimed by Kester 1996b).

Obvious counterexamples to the inflection requirement stem from the class of nondescriptive adjectives such *next* and *other*, or ordinal numerals. As outlined above, these adjectives can occur in an elliptical noun phrase, although they obviously do not carry any kind of morphological agreement feature. They are compatible with both singular and plural nouns, as the following examples illustrate:

(26) a. Inspect plants regularly and spray at **the first signs** of attack. (BNC, A0G 1356)

    b. So scratching the scalp is usually **the first sign** that a child has head lice. (BNC, A0J 1187)

(27) a. Unlike **the other men,** Peter did not suggest they meet again. (BNC, A0R 1278)

    b. **The other man** was still holding the sword upright as he went down. (BNC, A6N 461)

Number and genitive case are the only features that are morphosyntactically realized in the English noun phrase. But the example shows that there are adjectives that encode neither of these features and still function as licensors of noun ellipsis (see Chapter 2). Hence, inflection or strong agreement cannot be the licensing requirement.

A further problem, as pointed out by Panagiotidis (2003a), is the treatment of *one* as a lexical item that is inserted if the silent noun cannot be

30 *The Elliptical Noun Phrase in English*

licensed and identified. First of all, this assumption presupposes that *one* and the empty noun are in complementary distribution (as claimed, e.g., by Llombart-Huesca 2002). However, as illustrated in Chapter 2, there are a number of items such as *each, other, another,* or the ordinal numerals that select both:

(28) These are excellent biscuits. Can I have **another** (one)? (= example 3c, Chapter 2)

The more severe issue lies in the fact that the two nominal items, *one* and the silent noun, are considered to be subject to very different conditions. The parallels outlined above, however, suggest otherwise. A further problem arises from the Human and the Abstract Constructions. As will be argued in Chapter 4, these noun phrases contain (silent) empty nominal elements as well. It is the absence of a linguistic antecedent that brings about their [+human/+abstract] interpretation, that is, this rather "special" meaning does not derive from structural differences (examples 15–16 display a similar interpretation in terms of *one*; see Günther 2012 for a detailed discussion). This shows that, obviously, even a determiner plus an adjective regularly allows for the nominal position to remain empty (see also Panagiotidis 2003a), which also speaks against a strict licensing and identification requirement.

There are also conceptual objectives to a *pro* analysis of the ellipsis site. But they are not crucial for the present analysis and are circumvented with the proposal that renounces to an empty pronoun that needs formal licensing and identification, to be presented in Chapter 4. Therefore, they will not be addressed here. The reader is referred to Panagiotidis (2003a) for a detailed discussion.

Further issues arise out of the partitivity requirement that Lobeck introduces. They will be discussed in detail following the discussion of Sleeman's (1996) work, because this notion is taken to be licensing requirement in a number of approaches to noun ellipsis (Sleeman 1996; Sleeman 2003; Bouchard 2002; Gengel 2007; Alexiadou & Gengel 2009; Valois & Royle 2009; and López' 2000 discourse-linking condition) and thus merits closer investigation. Suffice it to say at this point that it is by no means clear in how far English morphosyntactically realizes partitivity. Even though there is undeniably a partitive construction in English, it is not clear to me how an element's ability to occur in such a construction is related to (strong) agreement.

3.3 SEMANTIC FEATURES—PARTITIVITY

3.3.1 Sleeman's (1996) Account for Noun Ellipsis

As has been pointed out, Sleeman (1996) argues against inflection or strong agreement as being the licensor of noun ellipsis (or *pro*) in French. She presents

Inflection, Focus, and Partitivity—Previous Accounts of Noun Ellipsis 31

instances of French adjectives, which, although they do inflect, do not allow for the noun to be omitted:

(29) An interesting lecture and some less interesting ones were given.

> *Malheureusement je n' ai pas entendu *l'intéressante.*
> unfortunately   I NEG have NEG heard   the interesting

> "Unfortunately, I have not heard the interesting one."
> (Sleeman 1996: 14)

Instead, Sleeman proposes that partitivity is the relevant feature in the licensing mechanism. A partitivity feature on the adjective licenses *pro* through proper government, no matter in which functional projection the adjective is generated, that is, the position of the adjective is not relevant for the licensing process. In this account, partitivity is not a strong agreement feature but a semantic one (contra Lobeck 1995). Partitivity is defined as "properly or improperly included within" (Sleeman 1996: 34), that is, it encodes set relations. Sleeman (1996: 34) presents the following examples to illustrate her understanding of those set relations and the closely-related concept of specificity (see Enç 1991).

(30) Several children entered my room. **Two girls** began to talk to me.

(31) What have you done today?—I have bought **two books**.

In example (30), the two girls are a subset of the several children that entered the room. According to Sleeman, the subset is interpreted as specific because it contains familiar information, that is, the referent is linked to what has been evoked earlier in the discourse. In example (31), on the other hand, the noun phrase does not receive a specific interpretation because it is not linked to familiar information.[8] Yet, Sleeman considers *two* to be a partitive element in this case as well, because "a subset is formed out of the superset denoting the kind" (1996: 34). Thus, *two books* refers to a subset of the class BOOK. It is worth mentioning that this subset does not necessarily have to be smaller than the superset; Sleeman accounts for elements such as *all* by incorporating improper inclusion into her definition.

Two types of elements with a partitive meaning are distinguished in this approach: D-partitives and N-partitives. The former, including quantifiers, numerals, and adjectives, such as *autre* "other," *prochain* "next," *suivant* "following," do not denote properties themselves. They are used to form a subset of the set denoted by the noun. These elements license noun ellipsis in both English and French. N-partitives, on the other hand, denote properties—they are intersective adjectives of quality, that is, the property they denote intersects with the denotation of the noun. These so-called "classifying adjectives" express "cognitively relevant notions which give them discriminating properties" (Sleeman 1996: 145), which, according

32   *The Elliptical Noun Phrase in English*

to Jones, help the addressee in "distinguishing the intended referent from other referents" (Jones 1993: 74).[9] These adjectives comprise color adjectives as well as antonymic pairs such as *big-small, old-new/young, good-bad,* that are the four major semantic adjective classes as defined by Dixon (1977). The discriminating meaning of these adjectives makes them partitive because they can "create subsets at a cognitive level" (Sleeman 1996: 35), which then evokes an association of *pro* with the existence of a superset. N-partitives only marginally license *pro* (for example, in English, where, according to Sleeman, color adjectives are the only ones among this group that allow for noun ellipsis), with French being an exception. In English, another partitive element is required with adjectives, namely *one.* Sleeman does not consider *one* the overt counterpart of the silent noun. Rather, she regards it as an element that licenses the silent empty noun via partitivity. Thus, in her account, *one*-insertion is an instance of noun ellipsis as well (see the discussion in the previous section), as has also been proposed by Kester (1996b).

Furthermore, there is a specificity requirement for the identification of *pro,* that is, the referent of the DP containing the ellipsis site must be linked to a discourse referent (see Enç 1991) in order to make the contents of the missing information recoverable. This requirement is established because indefinites containing an empty pronominal in object position are not grammatical in French. In these cases, the element *en,* which Sleeman considers an inherently specific overt NP pronoun, is required.

(32) a. *J' ai acheté *trois petites pro.*
     I have bought three small

    (Sleeman 1996: 69)

   b. J' en ai acheté *trois petites pro.*
     I of these have bought three small

   "Of these, I have bought three small (ones)."

In English, however, no overt specific pronoun such as French *en* is available. Thus, Sleeman suggests that in English specificity does not play a role in the licensing of noun ellipsis (1996: 52, 70). Support for this derives from indefinite elliptical noun phrases in object position:

(33) I have three *pro.* (Sleeman 1996: 51)

For reasons outlined in Section 3.1, the idea of an empty nominal element that needs licensing and identification is rejected in this work. Apart from this, some serious issues arise from positing a partitivity condition on noun ellipsis. The rather complex concept of partitivity is discussed in the next section.

3.3.2 The Notion of Partitivity

Even though a semantic feature can account for those licensors that are difficult to explain in an inflection-based approach, that is, the nondescriptive adjectives such as ordinals, *next*, and *other*, there are some severe issues with the notion of partitivity that need to be addressed.

First, as Sleeman points out, "the class of adjectives that can license pronominal NPs in French is still vague" (1996: 146). Furthermore, as will be pointed out within this section, the whole concept of partitivity is too vague to be applied to noun ellipsis. There are several different definitions to be found within each of the approaches that resort to this notion, and each of these definitions only captures some of the elements that allow for noun ellipsis. Sleeman, for example, presents a rather broad understanding of the term that comprises Lobeck's (1995) syntactic definition (partitive = combinable with a partitive PP) as well as specificity, and Bouchard puts forth a more narrow definition comprising only those elements that imply the existence of further referents. All three will be discussed in what follows.

3.3.2.1 The Syntactic Definition of Partitivity

Recall Lobeck's observation that the group of noun ellipsis licensors coincides with the group of elements that is able to occur with a partitive PP. Sleeman follows Lobeck in deriving a partitivity condition on noun ellipsis from this phenomenon (see also López 2000; Alexiadou & Gengel forthcoming). Two aspects need to be addressed here: the relationship between partitive noun phrases and elliptical ones, and the range of noun ellipsis licensors that this account captures.

Admittedly, there is a close relationship between the partitive construction and noun ellipsis, which seems to suggest a cause and effect relationship between the two phenomena. This relationship, however, is much more immediate than is assumed in the above accounts. As has already been suggested by Jackendoff (1977: 110ff), the partitive construction also contains a silent nominal element (see also Olsen 1987; Sauerland & Yatsushiro 2004; Fitzpatrick 2006). Jackendoff assumes a structure such as the following for partitive constructions:

(34) a. ART/Q PRO of NP

b. *those/few* PRO of the men

The empty noun ("PRO" in Jackendoff's account) is interpreted as UNIT via a Partitive Projection Rule (ibid.: 110). However, this has been criticized in the literature. López (2000: 191) points out that there are serious problems with this analysis; there is no overt counterpart for the silent noun, and in partitive constructions with mass interpretations (e.g., *most of the flour*),

34 *The Elliptical Noun Phrase in English*

the silent noun cannot be construed with a UNIT reading. This objection, however, only holds for a construal of the UNIT meaning for the empty element and is resolved easily if the empty noun is identified by the lexical noun in its PP complement, that is, that its meaning is recovered from the noun that follows it. What is more, there is an overt counterpart of the silent empty noun: *one* can be inserted, as the following examples demonstrate.

(35) Pietersburg in the conservative northern Transvaal was **the only one of the 15 regions** to record a majority "no" vote. (BNC, HLH)

(36) This is an ancient road, **the middle one of the three Roman roads** which went over the Pyrenees, . . . (BNC, FA2)

So, the partitive construction allows for the same elements that are licit in elliptical noun phrases because it also contains an empty nominal element, and, hence, is subject to the same conditions.

The case of *every* seems to be the prime example to establish cause and effect relations between the partitive construction and noun ellipsis. However, as Lobeck points out in a footnote, *every* can take a partitive PP:

(37) **Every one of the bills** we owe came in the mail today, and every one [e] is past due. (Lobeck 1995: 99; chap.3, n10)

She proposes that this might be "a kind of pronominalization rather than ellipsis" (ibid.). This is not convincing, however, because example (37) shows that *every* can have a partitive meaning. "Lexicalization *as everyone*," as suggested by Lobeck, does not hold either, because *one* could easily be modified by an adjective—*every single one of the bills*.[10] This very example supports the claim that the partitive construction involves noun ellipsis as well and is therefore subject to the same constraints (I will come back to this particular case in Section 4.2.2).

Finally, the definition of partitivity as "ability to take a partitive PP" does not comprise all elements that license noun ellipsis. As illustrated below (see Sleeman 1996: 156), this affects both D-partitives and N-partitives.

(38) *l'autre de ses livres
      the other of his books

(39) *le mien de ses livres
      the mine of his books

(40) *le nouveau de ses livres
      the new of his books

(41) trois des ses livres
      three of his books

Inflection, Focus, and Partitivity—Previous Accounts of Noun Ellipsis 35

These examples show that only some of the D-partitive elements, such as cardinal numerals, are actually partitive in the sense of the above definition.

3.3.2.2 Partitivity as a Semantic Feature

Sleeman suggests that "*partitive* does not necessarily have to mean 'combinable with a partitive PP'" (1996: 34). She makes reference to specificity, by pointing out that in Enç's (1991) understanding of specificity, a link between a set and a contextually active superset is established, which is reminiscent of the notion of partitivity.

(42) Tu   as   lu   tous ses livres? Non, je n'   ai   lu   que
     you have read   all   his   books? No, I   NEG have read than
     le   troisième.
     the third

"Have your read all his books? No, I have only read the third."
(Sleeman 1996: 33)

In this example, the elliptical noun phrase (or rather its referent) is a subset of a previously evoked set, that is, the books by a particular author. Sleeman points out that an elliptical phrase has to be linked to the context in order for *pro* to be recoverable. She claims that this requires specificity. The latter notion, however, is set apart from partitivity. As mentioned above, Sleeman considers the numeral in example (31) to be partitive but nonspecific, because *two* creates a subset of the class denoted by the noun, that is, the NP *two books* can be paraphrased as *two of the kind BOOK*. In other words, nouns can be considered to be supersets because they denote classes. Example (43) illustrates a partitive relation between an antecedent denoting a class and an elliptical noun phrase referring to a particular member of that class.

(43) Je n' aime pas *ces*   *robes*   *vertes*. Je prends *la bleue*.
     I NEG like   NEG these   dresses   green.   I take   the   blue

"I do not like the green dresses. I will take the blue one." (Sleeman 1996: 45)

In the above example, the first noun phrase in object position refers to objects of particular color—green dresses. The head noun denotes a class, that is, DRESS. The elliptical noun phrase introduces a further member of that class, specified according to the distinctive property of color. Therefore, a set relation obtains between the superset denoted by the noun and the two noun phrases (including the one containing the lexical noun that serves as antecedent). According to Sleeman (1996), in order for the elliptical noun phrase to be interpreted, *pro* has to be linked to the set, that is, the set relation has to be encoded by a partitive element due to the absence of the overt noun.

36   *The Elliptical Noun Phrase in English*

The set relation indicated in the previous example certainly obtains. It derives from the absence of lexical meaning on behalf of the noun; an empty noun "inherits" the meaning from an antecedent (either in the text-internal or the text-external world). The antecedent denotes a class, and the noun phrase containing the anaphoric form specifies a certain member of that class, which is distinguished according to a particular dimension (property, quantity, etc.). These different instantiations of the same kind can of course be subsumed under one term. In example (43) green dresses are dresses, and a blue dress is included in the category of dresses as well. The triviality of this matter underlines the weakness of this understanding of partitivity.

Sleeman's definition of partitivity as "properly or improperly included within" can be criticized along the same lines. Consider the following nominal expressions:

(44) all/some/many students

If *all, some,* and *many* pick out subsets of the set denoted by the noun (as claimed for *two books* in example [31]) and are partitive in that sense, partitivity coincides with quantification (see also Panagiotidis 2003b). If this is extended to adjectival modifiers, that is, if one claims that in examples such as *the green book,* a set relation is created because the adjective *green* picks out a subset of the book class, partitivity coincides with intersective modification.

However, this is problematic because nonintersective adjectives are licit modifiers of anaphoric nominal elements as well.[11] The following examples demonstrates that *alleged* and *fake,* the two prime examples of nonintersective adjectives, can be used with *one*:[12]

(45) Too late Yartek discovers <u>one key</u> to be the **fake one.** (BNC, F9Y)

(46) . . . <u>a real boss</u> as well as an **alleged one.** (COCA, 1991 ACAD)

In these examples, the items denoted by the anaphoric noun phrase are not subsets of the set denoted by the noun; a fake key is not a key and whether an alleged boss qualifies as boss is doubtful, too. This shows that intersective modification cannot be a licensing requirement.[13] Rather, it is restrictive modification that is the relevant aspect for the present phenomenon.

The cases where the elliptical noun phrase actually denotes a subset of the set denoted by the noun are also problematic for a partitivity condition on noun ellipsis. This is because, in English, there are three ways to realize an anaphoric nominal head: The head noun can be repeated (example 47), *one* can be used (example 48), or the position can remain empty (example 49).

(47) John and Mary (the two experimenters) show a child of three years of age <u>a red box</u> and **a blue box** and a pound coin. (BNC, A0T)

Inflection, Focus, and Partitivity—Previous Accounts of Noun Ellipsis 37

(48) Gentleman may have noticed that the citizens charter was not <u>a glossy blue document</u> but **a glossy red one.** (BNC, HHW)

(49) Should it be <u>the red carpet</u> or **the blue?** (BNC, H8A)

In each of the above cases, an anaphoric relation obtains and in each case, the previously mentioned set relation obtains. This reveals the weakness of the approach to partitivity put forth by Sleeman (the understanding of the notion as "subset of the kind denoted by the noun"). A partitivity-based approach cannot explain the different conditions on the use of *one* and the use of the silent noun. Rather, an understanding of partitivity as broad as this one does not entail more than the mere fact that, in cases of noun ellipsis, an anaphoric relation holds, that is, that the silent noun has the same content as its antecedent. To emphasize again, this claim most definitely does not make the wrong empirical predictions. It simply does not add much to the understanding of the licensing of the silent noun in English either, because it also applies to the use of *one* and, hence, does not capture the differences between the two nominal elements.

The set relation referred to gives rise to yet another issue. It is not clear how far the modifiers and determiners ensure that the set relation is recovered. If modifiers form a binary pair, one could claim that one modifier implies the other and hence signals that further potential referents must be available, which could then be considered to retrieve the link to the kind. For example, this holds for the use of discourse-referential modifiers, which, as pointed out in Chapter 1, signal that a referent must already be available in the discourse, or that a new one has to be construed. So, modifiers as used in example (50) indicate the presence of further referents:

(50) a. the next customer
     b. the first student

While the use of *next* implies that there have been other referents of the class of customers in the discourse before, the use of the ordinal *first* implies that there are more instances of the class of students to come. Therefore, in these cases, the link to a superset can be established. Modifiers like those in example (50) are actually considered partitive for this very reason in Bouchard's (2002) approach. Up to this point, the analysis is comprehensible. It can also be maintained for superlatives and probably covers cases of binary pairs of adjectival modifiers as well. For example, the use of *new* can imply that there is a referent that can be characterized as *old*, but it does not necessarily do so, as evident in the following examples:

(51) As Kirillov puts it, "I am killing myself to show my rebelliousness and **my new terrible freedom.**" (BNC, A18 1314)

38 *The Elliptical Noun Phrase in English*

(52) "I'll attack the pipes with **my new hammer.**" (BNC, A0D 857)

(53) I hadn't anticipated so much pressure in **my new life.** (BNC, FPJ 498)

As the examples show, this implication is only achieved if the modifier expresses a defining property and not an "accessory" one, which only provides additional, nondefining information. Thus, *new* does not always imply an *old* element; *new,* if used noncontrastively, means roughly "newly obtained". In example (51), *new terrible freedom* most likely does not imply that there is an old (terrible) freedom the speaker has experienced. Example (52) is ambiguous with respect to contrastiveness—the speaker could have possessed a hammer before, which would be the old hammer. In this case, a further referent would be implied. The noncontrastive reading, on the other hand, merely adds nondefining, additional information. Here, the hammer has been bought recently. No alternative is implied. Only in the third example the contrastive reading is the most likely one—the speaker must have been alive before, hence, there must be an old life.[14] What is in effect in these cases seems to be the requirement of contrastive focus, rather than partitivity.

It has to be pointed out that one of the prime licensors of noun ellipsis in English, the cardinal numerals, are not partitive in the above sense: The use of the noun phrase *two books,* for instance, does by no means imply the existence of further referents. The same holds for other elements such as *many, all, any, both, several,* and *some,* which were identified as licensors of noun ellipsis in Chapter 2:

(54) a. Her friends have got their results: **all/both** have passed. (= 1b, Chap.2)

    b. I need some dollar coins; have you got **some** I could borrow? (= 1c, Chap.2)

None of these elements implies the existence of further referents. A referring expression such as *the next student* presupposes that there also is previous student, as pointed out above. According to Bouchard, a partitive modifier "implies a superset in the domain of discourse from which a particular item (or items) are selected and ranked" (Bouchard 2002: 221). In terms of *next, previous,* and the ordinals, for instance, the items are ranked on a temporal scale. However, referring expressions such as *some dollar coins* or *all friends* do not signal that a further set is active; hence, these modifiers are not partitive in the above sense.[15]

To sum up, Sleeman's account for partitivity is very vague—what it boils down to is to saying that the silent element is interpreted via an antecedent. As pointed out above, a concept of partitivity that makes reference to the relation between referents and kinds definitely makes the correct predictions—antecedent and silent noun have the same meaning. Due to the fact

Inflection, Focus, and Partitivity—Previous Accounts of Noun Ellipsis 39

that the same conditions hold for the use of *one,* the differences in distribution between *one* and the silent noun cannot be accounted for. Sleeman offers a possible way out of the problem by postulating a partitive meaning for *one* as well—*one* licenses the empty pronominal via partitivity in analogy to the other modifiers. However, this is problematic for a few reasons: (a) this cannot explain how noun ellipsis can be licensed in mass noun phrases; (b) the licensors that can take both forms of nominals cannot be accounted for; and (c) it is not clear how far *one* can be considered to be partitive. Sleeman suggests that "prop word" *one* is partitive because numeral *one* is partitive (1996: 50f, n17). The two are certainly related etymologically, but they differ in a number of ways: Nominal *one* is inflected for number and it cannot be contrastively focused (see Dahl 1985), as illustrated in example (55).

(55) a. The list of themes and their varied fortunes is **a long one.** (BNC, A04 644)

b. *The list of themes and their varied fortunes is **a long ONE.**

Numeral *one,* in contrast, can be focused:

(56) a. **One law for the rich** and another for the poor, . . . (BNC, A05 265)

b. **ONE law for the rich** and another for the poor, . . .

Furthermore, both instances of *one* can co-occur; hence, they cannot be within the same position.

(57) Two small filters can be easier to hide than **one large one.** (BNC, C95 3077)

On the basis of these examples, the line of reasoning that nominal *one* has a partitive meaning has to be discarded.

A more narrow definition of partitivity as put forth by Bouchard (2002) does not capture a considerable number of licensors such as the cardinal numerals and *many, several, all,* and the like. This requires further assumptions in order to account for all instances of noun ellipsis in English. As will be argued in Chapter 4, there is a way to account for all licensors of the empty noun in English without postulating additional conditions and constraints.

3.4 INFORMATION STRUCTURE

A further strand of approaches to ellipsis integrates discourse-related notions such as topic, focus, and given versus new information (see, e.g., López 2000; Johnson 2001; Merchant 2001; Ntelitheos 2004; Winkler 2005, 2006; Sleeman

40 *The Elliptical Noun Phrase in English*

2003; Eguren 2010). The basic claims of information structural approaches to noun ellipsis are outlined in what follows.

3.4.1 Focus Projections

Corver and van Koppen (2009) assume that there is a nominal left periphery similar to that of the clause (see Rizzi 1997), which hosts discourse-related projections (see Aboh 2004) such as a focus phrase (FocP). The claim that focus is expressed in the nominal domain is motivated as follows. Prenominal adjectives usually display a certain order. Dixon defines the following classes, which are ordered as follows:

(58) VALUE > DIMENSION > PHYSICAL PROPERTY > SPEED > HUMAN PROPENSITY > AGE > COLOUR
(Dixon 1982: 16)

Scott (2002) shows that this rather strict order can be changed when an adjective is focused. This is evident in the following examples: Changing the word order in the premodifying string results in unacceptability, unless the adjective that is moved to the left receives focal stress.

(59) a. an alleged English baron
b. *an English alleged baron
c. an ENGLISH alleged baron

Scott (2002: 113) concludes that there is focus projection the adjective can move to. He proposes the following structure:

(60) $[_{DP}$ an $[_{FocusP}$ English$_j$ $[_{SpecSubj.CommentP}$ alleged $[[_{SpecNationality/OriginP}$ t$_j$ $[_{NP}$ baron]]]]]]
(Scott 2002: 113)

Corver and van Koppen (2009) consider focus to be the licenser of noun ellipsis. They distinguish between information (= presentational) focus and contrastive (= identificational) focus, following É. Kiss (1998), who defines the latter as follows:

Identificational Focus

An identificational focus represents the set of contextually or situationally given elements for which the predicate phrase can potentially hold; it is identified as the exhaustive subset of this set for which the predicate phrase actually holds. (É. Kiss 1998: 245)

Inflection, Focus, and Partitivity—Previous Accounts of Noun Ellipsis   41

Table 3.1 Adjectival inflection in Dutch

	Definite	Indefinite
Non-neuter, sg.	der klein-e goochelaar	een klein-e goochelaar
	the small-e magician	a small-e magician
Non-neuter, pl.	de klein-e goochelaars	klein-e goochelaars
	the small-e magicians	small-e magicians
Neuter, sg.	het witt-e konijn	enn wit-ø konijn
	the white-e rabbit	a white-ø rabbit
Neuter, pl.	de witt-e konijnen	witt-e konijnen
	the white-e rabbits	white-e rabbits

From Corver and van Koppen (2009: 8).

Contrastive focus has an identifying function, while information focus merely marks "the non-presupposed nature of the information conveyed" (ibid.: 251). According to Corver and van Koppen, contrastive focus licenses noun ellipsis. They present microvariation data from Dutch to prove their point and to argue against inflection/agreement-based accounts (such as Lobeck 1995 and Kester 1996b). The basic facts are summarized in what follows.

In Dutch attributive adjectives take the *-e* ending except for cases where the noun is indefinite, neuter, and singular, which is displayed in Table 3.1 (see also example 24 taken from Kester 1996a).

The agreement approach predicts that nouns in indefinite neuter singular noun phrases cannot be elided. This was shown in example (24), which is repeated in example (61):

(61) *een rod boek en een *groen* [e]   (= example 24)
     a red book and a green

It has been pointed out that some speakers find an example like (61) acceptable when the adjectival remnant takes the schwa ending. This observation is also made by Corver and van Koppen, who put forth the following example from colloquial Dutch:

(62) Over konijnen gesproken . . . (Talking about rabbits . . .)
     #Ik heb gisteren   *een zwart-e* zien lopen.
     I   have yesterday a   black-e seen walk

     "I saw a black one yesterday." (Corver & van Koppen 2007: 10)

The above suggests that inflection is the crucial factor for Dutch noun ellipsis. However, Corver and van Koppen claim that the *-e* suffix is also used as a focus marker, which is evident in a number of contexts. First,

42 *The Elliptical Noun Phrase in English*

the schwa ending can be used to emphasize the meaning of, for example, adverbs in Standard Dutch:

(63) a. verdomd   aardig
       damned   nice
  b. verdomd-e aardig
      damned-e nice
  (ibid.: 12)

Second, in Katwijk Dutch, it can emphasize the meaning of measuring phrases:

(64) a. 'n hóóp   water
     a heap   water
   "a lot of water"
  b. 'n hóóp-e water
     a heap-e water

"a LOT of water" (ibid.: 12f, example taken from Overdiep 1940)

Apart from the fact that noun ellipsis and focus (or emphasis) contexts share the same *-e* suffix, there is another interesting relation pertaining to cases where the remnant modifier does not take *-e,* that is, where the noun phrase is specified for indefinite, neuter, singular. Interestingly, in colloquial Dutch, the use of an uninflected adjective is acceptable when this adjective is contrastively focused:

(65) Jij   hebt een ZWART   konijn, maar ik heb een WIT.
    you have a   black$_{\text{STRESS}}$ rabbit but I have a   white$_{\text{STRESS}}$

"You have got a black rabbit, but I have a white one." (ibid.: 14)

Corver and van Koppen assume that the focused adjective is moved to a higher projection and the complement of FocP is phonologically deleted. In other words, the modifier "escapes" from the ellipsis site before the material is deleted.

3.4.2 Semantic Effects of Focus

Eguren (2010) also derives the distribution of silent nouns in Spanish from focus conditions. In his approach, however, it is the semantic implications of focus that are relevant for noun ellipsis, rather than the movement of a modifier to a focus projection. He puts forward the following condition:

> Contrastive focus identifies a relevant set or subset in a set of contextually or situationally given alternatives, and the focused constituent(s)

Inflection, Focus, and Partitivity—Previous Accounts of Noun Ellipsis 43

in the remnant cannot be (semantically) identical to the corresponding part(s) in the antecedent phrase.[16] (Eguren 2010: 443)

This has already been referred to in Section 3.1: In anaphoric relations that hold below noun phrase level, a restrictive modifier expresses defining properties. Thus, contrast is established between referents.

A short remark on semantic identity is in order at this point. Eguren shows that the noun phrase containing the nominal anaphora can have the same prenominal elements as the noun phrase bearing the antecedent.

(66) María ha leído dos artículos y Ana ha leído dos__.
"Mary has read two papers and Anna has read two __."
(Eguren 2010: 443)

In that case, however, these noun phrases are not coreferential either, which is why they are semantically nonidentical.

According to Eguren, a focused remnant serves a discourse-linking function, because by inducing alternatives it establishes a relation between a set and a superset, that is, "the inclusion relation presupposes the existence of a known descriptive class that is accessible to both speaker and hearer" (ibid.: 439). This allows for the noun's contents to be recovered.

This concept of focus is highly reminiscent of the notion of partitivity. First, the nondescriptive (discourse-referential) modifiers, such as *next, other,* or the ordinals (Sleeman's D-partitives) imply the existence of alternatives, that is, they are inherently contrastive (and thus function as licensors of noun ellipsis, according to Eguren). Second, the contrast condition (or non-identity condition) states that (at least) two referents are under consideration. Both the empty noun in elliptical noun phrases and the overt empty noun *one* receive their meaning from an antecedent, which may result in a subset relation. Therefore, the contrast condition and partitivity coincide.

Alexiadou and Gengel (forthcoming) claim that focus in elliptical noun phrases "may be conceived of as a by-product of partitivity." However, it seems more likely that the cause and effect relation works in the opposite direction. It was pointed out that with modifiers that constitute binary pairs a further referent (or an alternative) is implied only if the modifier is restrictive and adds defining information, which distinguishes the object in question from other items. This is precisely what contrastive focus does. The implication of an alternative, of another referent for which the property expressed in the modifier does not hold, establishes the relation to the set.

Eguren's approach is adopted in the present work: Contrast is considered to be the relevant requirement for noun ellipsis. It is a semantic feature related to the use of anaphoric elements on N-level. The exact relations between the different noun phrases and the entities they denote will be discussed in greater detail in Chapter 4. What is important at this point is

44 *The Elliptical Noun Phrase in English*

that this condition holds for the use of anaphoric nominal heads in general. Thus, it cannot be taken to account for the variation in terms of noun ellipsis versus the use of *one*. The explanation for this distribution has to be sought elsewhere.

3.5 *ONE* AS A CLASSIFIER

In more recent approaches to noun ellipsis, reference is made to nominal classification, which means that parallels are drawn between English and the so-called classifier languages. To a certain extent this suggests itself, because *one* as an empty element encodes number and is compatible with count antecedents only. This has motivated the claim that *one* is a classifier—comparable to numeral classifiers in classifier languages, such as Thai, Mandarin, or Japanese.

Alexiadou and Gengel (forthcoming), for example, consider *one* to be a classifier that licenses noun ellipsis via partitivity (see Sleeman's 1996 account for English *one*). They assume, following Borer (2005), that DP structure contains a classifier phrase (ClassP) dominating NP. This phrase has a dividing function—it introduces semantic singularity. ClassP is dominated by NumP, which hosts quantifiers and thus provides discrete quantification. There are two types of classifiers: They either mark formal gender (e.g., in Romance and Germanic languages, such as Dutch or German) or number (as in English). Alexiadou and Gengel follow Sleeman (1996) in that partitivity licenses noun ellipsis. English *one* is considered to be a classifier that is inserted into ClassP, and, being specified for [atom/partitivity], it licenses phonological deletion of NP. ClassP is specified as [±count]. The [-count] specification blocks the insertion of *one* into ClassP, which is why *one* is not used as a mass noun. DPs in Romance (Spanish and Italian) and other Germanic languages (German and Dutch) are also taken to host ClassP, but in contrast to English, the classifier itself is not overt.

A similar approach is provided by Llombart-Huesca (2002). She claims that *one* is a last resort procedure that gives phonological support to a number affix when no noun is present. Number morphology is needed for the semantic partitioning of count nouns. When the lexical (count) noun is missing, *one* needs to be inserted in order to make Num^0 overt. However, Llombart-Huesca's approach departs from the account by Alexiadou and Gengel, because she does not propose a classifier projection. In her approach, there are three functional projections in the nominal domain—DP, QP and NumP, with the latter hosting the classifying element. There are also differences in the licensing mechanisms. Llombart-Huesca argues that *one* cannot be the licenser of an empty category, because *one*-insertion takes place at a phonological level and thus is not available in the syntax as a licensor. She claims that lexical categories are not subject to licensing requirements, the latter only hold for functional categories. Being a functional head, an empty Num^0

Inflection, Focus, and Partitivity—Previous Accounts of Noun Ellipsis 45

must be licensed by strong agreement. The relevant features are those proposed by Lobeck (1995)—[+plural], [+partitive], and [+possessive]—realized on the element that immediately c-commands Num^0. The empty NP does not need licensing. It only needs a linguistic (or pragmatic) antecedent that allows for the missing lexical content to be recovered. If this condition is met, that is, if the NP is identified, it can remain silent. The number specification of the empty NP, however, cannot be recovered via an antecedent because the set referred to by the empty NP does not necessarily have the same number specification as the antecedent, as evident in example (67):

(67) I like this car and she likes those. (Llombart-Huesca 2002: 83)

Hence, being a functional element, the head associated with number specification has to be licensed—either by strong agreement features on the dominating head or by *one*-insertion. If licensing fails, for example, if it is blocked by an intervening adjective, as is the case in the following examples, *one* has to be inserted (Llombart-Huesca 2002: 79).

(68) [$_{QP}$ many [$_{AP}$ lazy [$_{NumP}$ one {pl} [$_{NP}$ ø]]]

Both papers present an interesting approach to noun ellipsis, and some of the crucial aspects will be adopted in Chapter 4. However, even though I believe that the proposals made here are on the right track, several points of criticism need to be mentioned.

The first should be obvious in light of the above: Note that again reference is made to the feature specification put forth by Lobeck (1995) and Sleeman (1996). It was argued in detail that a partitivity feature (either as a semantic or as an agreement feature) does not account for the distribution of *one* and the silent noun. A further problem relates to *one* as licensor: If *one* as a classifier licenses noun ellipsis, as Alexiadou and Gengel claim, then what licenses noun ellipsis in mass noun phrases? In a way, they circumvent this issue by postulating a classifier phrase for mass contexts as well. Its [-count] specification blocks *one*-insertion. But first, there is no independent motivation for this projection. Second, it is by no means clear how far this empty category should be endowed with a semantic feature required to license the silent noun. Furthermore, the view of *one* as a licensor is incompatible with the claim that *one* is an empty noun, too, which underlies this work.

3.6 SUMMARY

In the first section of this chapter, the properties of *one* and noun ellipsis were illustrated. The comparison revealed significant parallels between the two forms, which lead to the conclusion that both *one*-insertion and noun

46 *The Elliptical Noun Phrase in English*

ellipsis involve a descriptively empty nominal element, one remaining silent and the other being overt.

This provided a point of departure for the second part, where previous accounts of noun ellipsis were discussed. Three types of approaches have been identified: (a) those that consider inflectional properties and agreement features to be crucial for the licensing process of *pro* (Lobeck 1995; Kester 1996a, b); (b) those that relate licensing of noun ellipsis (*pro* in Sleeman's approach, or phonological deletion, e.g., in Alexiadou & Gengel forthcoming) to semantic partitivity being encoded on the licensor (Sleeman 1996; Bouchard 2002; Gengel & Alexiadou forthcoming); and (c) those that take informational structural properties of the nominal domain into consideration (Corver & van Koppen 2009; Eguren 2010). In terms of the latter, focus is either a syntactic feature, which triggers movement of the focused item to a higher projection where it "survives" the deletion process, or a semantic feature that links the empty element to a superset and hence allows for recoverability of the noun's contents.

It was argued that the aforementioned approaches do not provide satisfying answers to the crucial question of the differences in distribution of *one* and noun ellipsis and the relation between the two. The agreement-based approaches were discarded because noninflected items, such as *each, next, another,* or the ordinals, do license noun ellipsis in English. Lobeck (1995) captures the data by postulating that partitivity can be considered a strong agreement feature, based on the observation that partitive elements occur in a particular syntactic environment, the partitive construction. The parallels between this construction and noun ellipsis—both disallow for the same elements (see example 18)—supported this claim.

(69) a. The women came in and *each/*every* sat down.   (= example 18)

    b. *each* of the women

    c. **every* of the women

However, as pointed out above, these apparent parallels derive from the fact that the partitive construction also contains a silent empty noun. The nominal constructions in example (69) can be analyzed as follows:

(70) a. The women came in and *each* [e] sat down/ and **every* [e] sat down.

    b. *each* [e] of the women

    c. **every* [e] of the women

Therefore, the syntactic definition of partitivity cannot be maintained. Partitivity thus seems to be a semantic feature, as proposed by Sleeman (1996). The underlying assumption that the elliptical noun phrase refers to a subset of the class denoted by the antecedent noun was argued to be

Inflection, Focus, and Partitivity—Previous Accounts of Noun Ellipsis   47

intertwined with the contrast condition on the use of nominal anaphora: Different subsets of a class can only be established if the modifiers express defining properties that distinguish the subset from the superset. This suggests that contrast rather than partitivity should be considered the requirement for noun ellipsis—focus creates the subsets by indicating alternatives, and hence, partitivity is the effect rather than the cause.

Even though positing a contrast condition is justified, this cannot account for the use of *one* versus noun ellipsis. As Halliday and Hasan (1976) point out, the redefinition, that is, the expression of a distinguishing property, must also take place in terms of *one*-insertion. Hence, an account for the empty noun in English must be sought along different lines.

The major problem in the approaches discussed is that noun ellipsis and the use of *one* are considered to be two separate phenomena. The idea that *one* is inserted whenever the empty noun cannot be licensed is on the wrong track. Rather, we are dealing with one phenomenon with the same underlying semantico-pragmatic conditions (such as contrast, recoverability of the noun, etc.), as suggested by the data presented in Section 3.1. The choice between *one* and the silent empty noun will be argued to be determined by morphosyntactic factors—the absence of inflectional properties on the adjective results in the latter being unspecified for countability. The choice between *one* and the empty noun is governed by the expression of countability. This choice, however, is determined by the surface order of the noun phrase's constituents, that is, *one* is not inserted if the licensing process of the silent noun fails. Rather, *one* is deleted under certain conditions. A detailed account will be developed in Chapter 4. It combines crucial aspects of the above analyses, in particular the ideas pertaining to contrast and focus and inflection-based approaches, which, as will become evident in Section 4.3, also relate to nominal classification.

4 Conditions on Noun Ellipsis in English

This chapter develops a novel account of noun ellipsis in English. It presents a detailed description of the licensing conditions as well as the structure of the elliptical noun phrase. The first licensing requirement to be laid out in detail is the contrast condition. It applies to both empty nouns, that is, the silent noun in elliptical noun phrases and the overt empty noun *one*. A countability requirement, the second condition to be discussed, will be shown to determine the distributional differences between the two nominal forms: If the element preceding the nominal form is specified for [±count], the empty noun remains silent because it expresses redundant information. This adjacency requirement of licensor and ellipsis site implies that the choice between *one* and silent form is determined on the surface, that is, by linear order. Even though the analysis is also compatible with a lexicalist view of the mass-count distinction, it will be implemented within a structural approach, in which countability is assumed to be a property of the entire noun phrase. *One* will be argued to be the phonological form of an empty noun hosting number morphology, which is only available in count noun phrases and hence has a function comparable to numeral classifiers in the so-called classifier languages.

Section 4.1 presents the notion of contrast relevant for the use of empty nominal forms. Section 4.2 deals with countability as a factor determining the choice between silent empty noun and *one*. It shows that prenominal elements that do not require *one* are specified for countability, whereas elements that need *one* are not specified with regard to this distinction. In addition, borderline cases and apparent problems, such as the use of *every* with *one*, are discussed. The structure of the elliptical noun phrase is dealt with in Section 4.3, where it is shown how the findings from Section 4.2 can be combined with a structural approach to the mass-count distinction, drawing on analogies to noun ellipsis in classifier languages. In a final step, the analysis is extended to German. Section 4.4 summarizes the chapter.

4.1 EMPTY NOUNS AND CONTRAST

As indicated throughout this work, contrast plays a crucial role in noun ellipsis. This notion is referred to in two types of contexts. First, contrast

Conditions on Noun Ellipsis in English   49

is often taken to be a pragmatic condition that allows for adjectives being used without *one*: "when a sharp contrast [is] presented, *one* may be omitted" (Bouchard 2002: 225; see Chapter 2). Second, contrast is considered to be a semantic condition on the licensing of noun ellipsis (see Chapter 3), that is, a requirement that holds for any elliptical noun phrase and not only for those containing adjectives. In Chapter 3, it was pointed out that this requirement applies to both the silent noun and *one*, because they are both empty nominal elements.[1]

This section is meant to clarify the relation between contrast and noun ellipsis in order to provide a full picture of the conditions on the phenomenon in English, as well as to lay the foundations for the corpus analysis to be presented in Chapter 5.[2]

Broadly speaking, contrast refers to some kind of opposition; it involves a comparison of elements with respect to a property in which those elements differ. Obviously, this is a rather vague understanding of the term, but finding an exact definition of contrast is by no means trivial, as the ongoing discussion in the literature indicates (for an overview, see Molnár 2006 and Repp 2010), and, therefore, is beyond the scope of this work.

What is crucial for the present purpose is that contrast is closely related to focus, where a set of potential alternatives is generated (see Rooth 1992 on alternative semantics). This is summarized in Krifka's definition of focus:[3]

> Focus indicates the presence of alternatives that are relevant for the interpretation of a linguistic expression. (Krifka 2007: 18)

This effect can be illustrated with an example:

(1) What did you buy yesterday?

> I bought a hat.
> (Kenesei 2006: 148)

In the noncontrastive reading, the question inquires about what the addressee bought. The answer only conveys information about an object, *a hat*, that fits the description. There is no information about further objects that were purchased—the addressee might have bought other objects and the answer would still be valid. Hence, no alternatives are given. However, in the contrastive reading, which is possibly better captured in a cleft construction, *It's a hat that I bought,* implies that further objects could have been bought, but the hat was the only member of that set that was actually picked. Hence, alternatives that may have been situationally specified (e.g., the addressee may have mentioned that she intended to buy a hat, a shirt, and so on) are rejected.

Throughout this work reference has been made to the contrast condition and the non-identity condition. They apply both to ellipsis and *one*-insertion, which is in line with the claim that *one* is the overt counterpart of the silent

50   *The Elliptical Noun Phrase in English*

form of the empty noun. It was pointed out that various authors working within different frameworks assume that the antecedent noun phrase has to differ from the anaphoric one. These differences will be investigated in what follows. As it is somewhat difficult to find proper instances of noun ellipsis, the illustrations are based on *one*-insertion. This is not problematic because the same conditions apply.

Eguren (2010) and Giannakidou and Stavrou (1999) put forward a generalization that affects prenominal modifiers: The one modifying the antecedent cannot be identical to the one modifying the empty nominal form. This definition can be illustrated with examples such as the following:

(2) WHY are you less likely to get caught speeding in <u>a black car</u> and most likely in **a red one?** (BNC, CH5 3358)

(3) "I'm the entertainments director," Mandy repeated, missing the undertows that were now thick in the air around her, as <u>dark blue eyes</u> met **light blue ones** and clashed like hot air hitting cold. (BNC, JY6 519)

In example (2), the contrastive relation holds between the different adjectival modifiers. As example (3) shows, parts of the modifying string can be identical if other parts differ. This difference is not necessarily expressed prenominally, it can be encoded in a post-modifier (the definite article itself is noncontrastive; see Section 4.2.3 for further discussion).

(4) Yeah you like, you, he likes **the one that without sugar** and I like **the one with sugar.** (BNC, KCP 4907)

(5) The difficulty with writing it down was that it became real to the extent of being in a book, there were two lives, **the one in the book** and **the one which he lived to collect the details for the book one;** he could go further in his head than on the page, the words slowed him down. (BNC, HDC 1367)

As Halliday and Hasan (1976) point out, if the antecedent noun phrase and the anaphoric one refer to the same entity, the entire anaphoric phrase is replaced by a pronoun, not just the nominal head:

> In reference there is a total referential identity between the reference item and that which it presupposes, nothing is added to the definition. In substitution there is always some redefinition. Substitution is used precisely where the reference is not identical, or there is at least some new specification to be added . . . the new definition is contrastive with respect to the original one. (Halliday & Hasan 1976: 95)

This is evident in the use of the personal pronouns in contexts such as in example (6) and example (7).

Conditions on Noun Ellipsis in English 51

(6) In Britain it has long been believed that if <u>a black cat</u> crosses your path or enters your house it will bring you good fortune. (BNC, BMG 1648)

(7) Tim: I saw <u>a black cat</u> on the step.

Dorothy: Did you?

Tim: But **he** went away.

(BNC, KBW 17664–6)

In these examples, a referent is introduced into the discourse with the help of an indefinite noun phrase. Then, a personal pronoun is used to anaphorically refer to the same referent again. A noun phrase where the anaphor only holds on the nominal level would be infelicitous in these contexts as the following modified versions of examples (6) and (7) indicate:

(6') In Britain it has long been believed that if <u>a black cat</u> crosses your path or enters your house **#the black one** will bring you good fortune.

(7') I saw <u>a black cat</u> on the step.
#But **the black one** went away.

In a slightly adapted setting, the use of a noun phrase containing *one* would be felicitous:

(7") I saw <u>several cats</u> on the step.
But **the black one** went away.

Here, there are several instances of the class CAT available in the discourse, that is, there is more than one referent qualifying as cat. Furthermore, it is relevant that there are also cats that are not black. The use of *one* in a definite noun phrase with the modifier *black* signals that one of the cats under consideration was black. The modifier expresses a defining property that distinguishes the referent in question from the other referents in that set. The anaphoric noun phrase in this case is not coreferential to the one hosting the antecedent. Rather, the referent of the anaphoric one is a subset of the referents introduced by the antecedent noun phrase.

The above discussion indicates that the use of an empty nominal element presupposes the existence of alternatives, but this does not account for the following examples:

(8) Dorothy: Is that <u>a nice cat</u>, do you stroke it?

Tim: <-|-> Yeah.

Christopher: <-|-> Yes <-|-> it is **a nice one** mummy.
(BNC, KBW 17674–6)

52   *The Elliptical Noun Phrase in English*

(9) Rosemary: and I thought to myself that blooming cat's after them and er it kept on for a long time and then, so I opened the window and looked out \<pause\> <u>a big black cat</u> was here \<pause\> \<unclear\> \<pause\> where's <u>the big black cat</u> coming from?

John: Dunno I haven't seen \<unclear\>

Rosemary: Yeah **a big, big black one** \<pause\> well it looked black in \<pause\> it was in the early hours of this morning, you know, when the birds start \<pause\> flying about.

(BNC, KDS 964–6)

(10) But <u>a new caravan</u> starts from eleven thousand eight hundred. That's the price of **a new one**. (BNC, KCN 4022–4)

In all three examples the modifiers of *one* and those of the antecedents are identical. There is not even a redefinition in the sense of Halliday and Hasan, apart from the intensifying use of a doubled adjective in example (9). The reason why the speakers do not make use of pronouns here relates to the syntactic roles of these phrases. In example (8), both are predicates, and neither of them is referential. One speaker inquires about a property of that cat by asking whether it qualifies as nice. The other speaker confirms this by using the anaphoric expression with a repetition of the modifier that predicates the defining property of the referent. Similarly, in example (8) the noun phrase containing *one* functions as a predicate. Thus, the two noun phrases are also not coreferential. The third example differs in that the anaphoric phrase is not used predicatively; it does refer as the use of the personal pronoun *they*, as the second anaphoric noun phrase indicates. However, both the antecedent and the two anaphoric phrases do not refer to a particular individual, that is, there is no specific new caravan. These expressions are interpreted generically, that is, they refer to the whole group of new caravans. The modifier in these examples expresses a defining property again—*new* establishes a contrast to used exemplars of the class denoted by the noun.

The data suggest that if the modifier is the same in antecedent and anaphoric noun phrases, the latter do not refer to the same entity, that is, they are not coreferential (but generic reference is allowed). The question arises whether they can ever refer to the same specific entity. Dahl (1985) presents an example illustrating that they can.[4]

(11) A: Would you like me to change <u>the pictures in your room</u>?

B: No, I think I'd like to keep **the same ones**.

(Dahl 1985: 67f)

Conditions on Noun Ellipsis in English 53

Thus, elliptical noun phrase and the one containing the antecedent can be coreferential. Yet, in these examples the modifiers are not identical.

In light of the above discussion, it is evident that Halliday and Hasan's claim can be confirmed. If the antecedent phrase and the anaphoric phrase are coreferential, a redefinition takes place, that is, a new aspect is added to the original description. If the two are identical (apart from the nominal form, of course), then they do not refer to the same entity. This is presumably what Eguren has in mind when he states that "the focused constituent(s) in the remnant cannot be (*semantically*) identical to the corresponding part(s) in the antecedent phrase" (Eguren 2010: 443, emphasis added). He presents the following examples from Spanish:

(12) María ha comprador <u>*estos libros*</u> y Ana ha comprador **estos** __.

   "Mary has bought these books and Ann has bought these __."

(13) María ha leído <u>dos artículos</u> y Ana ha leído **dos** __.

   "Mary has read two papers and Ann has read two __."
   (Eguren 2010: 443)

Here, the two noun phrases do not refer to the same entities, although they contain the same demonstrative and numeral.

As pointed out, set relations are frequently referred to in accounts of noun ellipsis. The following relations and configurations can be identified on the basis of the above discussion.

(14) **Partitive relations**

   The referent(s)[5] of the anaphoric noun phrase(s) is/are included in the set established via the antecedent noun phrase. The restrictive modifier in the anaphoric phrase(s) denotes a defining property.

   Examples
   a. For my part, I think there was the temptation to cause myself pain: to call up the memory of <u>so many anguished partings at railway stations</u>, so much less anguished (it seemed now) than **the final one**. (BNC, AMC 223)
   b. It may involve visiting <u>several firms</u> before you find **the right one**. (BNC, A0X 834)

(15) **Different members of the same class**

   The antecedent noun denotes a class. Both the referent of the antecedent noun phrase and the referent(s) of the anaphoric phrases(s) are different members of that class. The modifiers denote defining properties by which those members can be distinguished.

54   *The Elliptical Noun Phrase in English*

Examples

a. Do you take out <u>a new loan</u> to pay off **the old one**? (BNC, A7N 554)

b. There is a widespread tendency in social science and in more popular discussions of opinion/attitude surveys to assume that <u>a large sample</u> provides some automatic guarantee of reliable results, while **a small one** promises unreliability. (BNC, EBR 483)

(16) **Referential identity**

An adjective denoting identity, such as *very* or *same*, is used in the anaphoric NP.

Examples

a. "Of course we thought about <u>political problems</u>, but everyone in Israel suffers from **the same ones**," says Igor, a railway engineer studying at the Mevasseret ulpan. (BNC, A8P 92)

b. The first thing they'd do if they captured one would be to hack off <u>the two forefingers of each hand</u>, **the very ones our archers used to pull a long bow**. (BNC, HH5 2644)

In addition, the noun phrases can be lexically identical as long as they are not coreferential. This applies if there are different referents or if at least one of the phrases is nonreferential. Generic reference seems to be licit, however. In all cases, the modifier expresses a defining property, which indicates alternatives. This was evident in example (7), where the use of the contrastive modifier (the *black one*) was only felicitous if the initially established set contains more than one referent (several cats). At the same time the use of the modifier in that anaphoric phrase indicates that there are entities that do not display that very property, that is, there are cats that have colors other than black. In the same vein, the use of an anaphoric nominal form in example (17) is only felicitous in contexts where there are other potential items of the same kind but of a different color.

(17) Hey, look! A black one! And another black one!

This is precisely what focus does. It indicates alternatives (note that the modifiers in example 17 bear contrastive stress).

Obviously, these alternatives are required in noun ellipsis contexts. Eguren provides examples of modifiers for which no opposite notions are available. These are not allowed in Spanish noun ellipsis constructions:

(18) Eso es un puro *(disparate).

"That is sheer nonsense."
(Eguren 2010: 449)

Conditions on Noun Ellipsis in English 55

This also indicates why partitivity is such a prominent concept: With the help of contrast, an entity is linked to a set of alternatives. Hence, a partitive relation (in the broadest sense) holds between items. As argued in Chapter 3, partitivity construed in this way is a side effect of focus (see also Eguren 2010).

4.2 NOUN ELLIPSIS VERSUS *ONE*-INSERTION

The contrast condition described above applies to both types of empty nouns. To shed light on the properties a licensor of the silent empty noun (i.e., noun ellipsis) must have, a closer look at the properties of *one* proves insightful. *One* differs from the silent empty noun in three respects. First, it has a phonological form; second, it hosts number morphology, that is, it is either singular or plural; and third, it is incompatible with a mass reading (see, e.g., Jespersen 1933). The latter is illustrated by example (19). *One* cannot have noncount antecedents; hence, a different strategy—noun ellipsis—must be used (Stirling & Huddleston 2002: 1515).

(19) a. *The advice you gave was more useful than the one I received from the Dean.
  b. The advice you gave was more useful than that which I received from the Dean.
  c. Your advice was more useful than the Dean's.

A glance at the prenominal elements in elliptical noun phrases indicates that number has its share in the licensing process: Elements such as the cardinals, as well as *both, several, a few, many, each*, and the like, do not allow for *one* and they are specified for number (singularity or plurality), which requires a look at the properties of number. The following quote from Bouchard explicates the importance of number in the nominal domain.

> The typical role of a nominal expression is to provide information to identify one of the actants of the event described by the sentence, i.e., a noun is the canonical realization of an actant in grammar. A common noun expresses a property—for instance "dog"—which defines a set whose extension corresponds to the ideal generated by the totality of the individuals—in this case, the totality of dogs. [. . .] The property of a common noun is not atomized, i.e., it does not define the quantity of individuals to which it may be applied, and is thus seen as a mass: it applies in an undifferentiated way to all individuals of the set, to the set itself and to all its subsets. This grammaticalization of a set by an N induces interpretations that do not distinguish between mass-count or singular-plural. So a *significant* for TOMATO

56 *The Elliptical Noun Phrase in English*

at this level of grammaticalization does not distinguish between a tomato, the tomato, some tomatoes, the tomatoes, or tomato as a mass. (Bouchard 2002: 40)

Number provides access to individuals, as it can atomize the property denoted by the noun (see also Alexiadou et al. 2007 for a summary of Bouchard's account). Hence, it is of prime importance to the referential system. Now, in terms of noun ellipsis, the element bearing number is absent from the structure. Bouchard assumes that this is the reason why noun ellipsis is subject to strict restrictions in English: Number is coded on the head noun and, therefore, this head cannot easily be elided.[6] The nature of the elements not requiring *one*, as well as the distribution of *one* itself, suggests that in the absence of a noun, number needs to be expressed on another item. As appealing as this explanation may look at first sight, it does not capture a number of items, such as the discourse-referential adjectives. As pointed out in Section 3.2.3, these do not convey number information because they can modify both singular and plural nouns. Examples (26) and (27) in Chapter 3 are repeated below.

(20) a. Inspect plants regularly and spray at **the first signs** of attack. (BNC, A0G 1356)

    b. So scratching the scalp is usually **the first sign** that a child has head lice. (BNC, A0J 1187)

(21) a. Unlike **the other men,** Peter did not suggest they meet again. (BNC, A0R 1278)

    b. **The other man** was still holding the sword upright as he went down. (BNC, A6N 461)

Due to the fact that these elements do allow for noun ellipsis, the expression of number cannot be the relevant licensing condition, at least not the only one. The above quote from Bouchard signals that number not only identifies participants in an event, it also distinguishes mass and count interpretations.

As Olsen (1987), Kester (1996b), and Barbiers (2005) point out, noun ellipsis in English is related to a [count] feature. The data suggest that it is indeed this distinction that determines the distribution of the two empty nouns. If a prenominal element is [-count], that is, if it is only compatible with mass, *one* cannot be inserted because it is a count noun. This holds for elements such as *much* and *little*.

(22) They learn that a cake takes lots of <u>mixing</u>, but muffins **very little.** (COCA, 2010 NEWS)

Conditions on Noun Ellipsis in English 57

If, on the other hand, an element is [+count], that is, compatible with count interpretations, *one* need not be used.

(23) Do you want more <u>tapes</u> for them to take away? I've got **ten**. (BNC, FM2)

(24) But, the choice is merely between buying one <u>board game</u> or **buying several**. (BNC, BNP)

(25) I have four <u>cigarettes</u> left and I need **many more**. (BNC, ADA)

With elements unspecified with respect to countability, such as property-denoting adjectives, which are compatible with mass and count structures, the use of *one* is required.[7]

(26) . . . the larger <u>market towns and cities</u> have grown in size much faster than **the small ones**. (BNC, B1H)

(27) For today's <u>kites</u> have one unique quality which made **the old ones** so tiresome to fly. (BNC, K35)

The subsequent sections show that this generalization covers a greater number of noun ellipsis licensors than the previous accounts.

4.2.1 Mass-Count Properties of the Licensors

In Chapter 2 it was pointed out that the following elements can only take a silent empty noun: cardinal numerals, plural demonstratives, genitives (phrasal and determinative), as well as the determiners and quantifiers *all, both, any, none, much, little, enough, sufficient, some, several, (a) few, many, more, most, less, plenty.* and *a lot.* They do not readily allow for *one*-insertion, unless, of course, a modifier intervenes.[8] As outlined above, most of these items are either compatible with a count or a mass reading. Whereas this is rather straightforward in terms of, for example, the cardinals, that is, elements that count, it is somewhat less obvious when it comes to discourse-referential modifiers such as the ordinals, *(an)other*, or *(n)either*. However, these items presuppose that entities are countable, too. This is evident in examples such as the following, where the mass interpretation of a noun, *beer*, that readily allows for both a count and a mass reading, is blocked once one of the above modifiers is used:

(28) When the first beer had gone they ordered **another**, and turned to survey the inn. (BNC, GWF 3108)

(29) She finished most of her second beer, then ordered **a third**. (COCA, 2005 FIC)

58 *The Elliptical Noun Phrase in English*

The use of *one* being licit in examples of this kind provides evidence for the count interpretation.

(30) Whereas he drank **the first beer** slowly, he wolfs **the next one** in an instant, thoughtlessly and without passion. (COCA, 2000 MAG)

(31) He didn't want **another beer**, hadn't wanted **the first one**. (COCA, 2004 MAG)

This naturally follows from the properties of these adjectives; the use of an ordinal, for example, implies a sequence of referents. Thus, these elements can only interact with manageable, well-defined portions. The same applies to the adjectives *next, last, previous,* and *following.* Now, the link to partitivity in the sense of Bouchard (2002) becomes obvious. These adjectives have a special status in that they do not attribute properties but serve a discourse-referential function, as pointed out in Chapter 1. According to Rijkhoff, discourse-referential modifiers "provide the addressee with information about the referent as a discourse entity" (Rijkhoff 2008: 798). The use of *other,* for example, directs the addressee to identify a second member of a previously established set of referents. Therefore, these elements imply that there is more than one referent of the same kind—in this respect, they are partitive. But in light of the above, it becomes clear that their ability to occur in elliptical noun phrases does not derive from the set relations they establish, but from the fact that, as soon as a further referent of the same kind is implied, there are at least two—hence, they are countable. Superlatives can be integrated into the account in a similar vein; they also imply the existence of alternatives.[9]

In Section 2.1.2, it was mentioned that the status of the singular demonstrative with respect to its ability to license noun ellipsis is somewhat dubious. Although it seems to be acceptable with noun ellipsis, Payne and Huddleston (2002) claim that it is more likely to license *one*-insertion.

The borderline status of these items can also be accounted for with reference to the mass-count distinction. The problem lies in them not being specified for countability. It is clear that singular demonstratives can determine countable entities, but, according to Allan (1980), they are also compatible with mass readings. He states that the noun phrases in the following expressions are uncountable:[10]

(32) a. This water is cold.

b. That flour's damp.

(Allan 1980: 543)

This underspecification in terms of countability explains why singular demonstratives are usually not considered to be licensors of noun ellipsis.

Conditions on Noun Ellipsis in English   59

The reason for them being listed as licensors, I believe, lies in the construal of the examples given, repeated here as example (33).

(33) a. This copy is clearer than that (one). (= example 4, Chapter 2)
        (Stirling & Huddleston 2002: 1511)

    b. That sausage has only 25% percent meat, but this has 90%.
        (Payne & Huddleston 2002: 414)

In both examples, the antecedent is determined by a singular demonstrative as well. These two demonstratives—being proximal and distal—form a contrastive pair. This results in a contrast of different members of the same class (denoted by the noun), which makes it possible to access well-defined portions, that is, the hearer is able to identify individual referents. Thus, under certain conditions, pragmatics can override structural restrictions. The role of pragmatics will be discussed in greater detail in terms of property-denoting adjectives in Chapter 5.

There is one aspect that seems to pose a problem for the account developed here. Some elements that license noun ellipsis seem to be unspecified in terms of countability. *All, plenty, more, most, some,* and *any,* for example, are compatible with mass and count readings (see Borer 2005: 119), and the same holds for *enough* and *sufficient.* However, as will be argued in Section 4.3.2, the requirement for countability to be expressed is a purely structural one. There is no pragmatic need to disambiguate mass and count readings, because the hearer knows whether the elliptical noun phrase refers to a countable entity or not, due to the antecedent. When these elements are construed with a count reading, they bear a [+plural] feature. When they are used in a mass context, that is, with a noun not inflected for number, the feature is absent, which results in a mass reading. Hence, these elements have a specification for countability that depends on the syntactic context in which they are used; they can be [+count] or [-count], depending on whether the noun phrase denotes a mass or a countable entity.

A more severe problem is caused by the ability of prenominal genitive elements to license an empty noun. Furthermore, they even block *one*-insertion, at least in Standard English (see Chapter 2). However, they do not express countability. I do not have an explanation for this and leave this open.

4.2.2 The Nature of *Every One*

Another issue that needs to be addressed is the fact that *every* does not license noun ellipsis, although it is specified for [+count] (see, e.g., Borer 2005). Hence, one would expect *every* to pattern similarly as *each,* another distributive quantifier, in the licensing of noun ellipsis. However, *each* and *every* display structural differences in a variety of contexts, such as in the

60 *The Elliptical Noun Phrase in English*

ability to occur as floating quantifiers and in the interaction with negation (see Beghelli & Stowell 1997; Fitzpatrick 2006).

As pointed out, contrast is a crucial aspect in noun ellipsis contexts. Eguren (2010), who attributes the licensing of noun ellipsis in Spanish to focus (see Chapter 3), shows that Spanish does not allow for *todos* "every" to be used without noun:

(34) a. Todos __ respetan a su professor.

"All __ respect their teacher."

b. *Todo __ respeta a su professor.

"Every __ respects his teacher."(Eguren 2010: 446)

Eguren accounts for this phenomenon as follows: Elements such as *todos* "all" quantify over contextually relevant sets, while the universal quantifier *todo* "every" quantifies over the entire class denoted by the noun. Therefore, it cannot identify an alternative set in terms of contextually given alternatives. In other words, *every* cannot be contrastively focused, in contrast to *all* or *each*. This might be the reason for its incompatibility with an empty noun.

So far, *every* has been treated as an element that allows for *one*-insertion only. The discussion of the partitivity condition in Chapter 4 illustrated that this element is often used to argue for a partitivity constraint on noun ellipsis, because of its distributional properties. Lobeck's (1995: 93) example is repeated here for convenience.

(35) a. The women came in and each/*every sat down.

b. each of the women

c. *every of the women

According to the partitivity approaches to noun ellipsis, *one*-insertion in the partitive construction makes the use of *every* licit.

(36) Those five gates of hell, he'd be put through **every single one of them**. (BNC, C86 1000)

If the idea that the mass-count properties on prenominal elements determines whether an overt empty has to be used or not is on the right track, either *both* anaphoric nominal elements (the silent empty noun and *one*) should be licit here or *none* of them. Due to *every* being specified as [+count] but [-plural], one would expect it to take both forms. As it definitely does not license a silent noun (the literature is consistent on this matter; furthermore, there are no instances of *every* + silent noun in the BNC), this is probably due to its semantics, as pointed out above. However, if *every* does

Conditions on Noun Ellipsis in English   61

not qualify as contrastive, *one* should not be licit either, given that both anaphoric forms are subject to the same semantic-pragmatic constraints.

Interestingly, elements differ with respect to their ability to license a stressed version of *one*. As Dahl (1985) shows, *every* only allows for the stressed version—*every single ONE*. Descriptive adjectives, on the other hand, do not allow for stressed *one*.

(37) A: Which t-shirt should I wear?

 B: Wear the
  a. BLUE one.
  b. *blue ONE.
  (Dahl 1985: 18)

This raises the question why does *every* only allow for stressed *one*, whereas adjectives can only occur with the unstressed version. There is a good reason to assume that in the case of *every* no "real" *one*-insertion obtains, that is, we are not dealing with the overt empty noun here. This is demonstrated in what follows.

First, the following data show that *every one* can be followed by a lexical noun.

(38) But there are seven male to **every one female tenured academic psy-chologist**, . . . (BNC, CMR 88)

(39) . . . (customers will buy two Aga-saga paperbacks **for every one hard-back.**) (BNC, K5F 1550)

(40) For every one person who succeeds there are likely to be dozens and dozens who fail . . . (BNC, AD0 74)

(41) There may be as many as 15 gaelic players for every one rugby player. (BNC, CKA 436)

Hence, a nominal position is available following *one*. This shows that *one*, in these cases, functions as a numeral. Indeed, further examples show that other numerals are licit in this position.

(42) . . . there is one soldier for **every two banana workers.** (BNC, HH3 13964)

(43) Statistics show that one in **every three company directors aged 40** will die before reaching age 65. (BNC, AYP 3199)

(44) . . . and two out of **every three street lights** are extinguished for economy . . . (BNC, HR7 1145)

62   *The Elliptical Noun Phrase in English*

(45)   So **every ten point six minutes,** another engine comes off the end. (BNC, G5B 129)

In light of these examples, *one* has to be considered a numeral rather than an empty noun. The numeral is then followed by a silent empty noun. The structure for *every one* thus looks as follows:

(46)   every ONE __

This idea gets support from the following data. The position following the numerals in examples (42) to (45) does not have to be filled by an overt nominal element as demonstrated in examples (47) to (50). Hence, example (46) is an instance of the more general structure *every cardinal* __.

(47)   . . . covering one patient in **every eight** in the country (BNC, K5M 619)

(48)   . . . cancer is still the major killer of children, with one in **every 600** getting some form of the disease. (BNC, G36 648)

(49)   . . . and the Commission will last for 10 years, to be reviewed **every three.** (BNC, J2X 141)

(50)   . . . we'll give him half an ounce of brandy every two hours, and twenty drops of laudanum **every four.** (BNC, EFW 256)

However, Dahl (1985) argues against treating stressed *one* as a numeral. Some adjectives, such as *favorite*, also allow for stressed *one*. Dahl points out that although numerals can generally occur in post-adjectival position, this slot cannot be filled by numeral *one*:

(51)   a.   Those are my favorite two TV shows.

     b.   *That's my favorite one TV show.

       (Dahl 1985: 31)

However, instances of numeral *one* in post-adjectival position are attested in the BNC.

(52)   . . . the smallest penis encountered in the Kinsey survey was **a mere one inch** long. (BNC, BP4 499)

(53)   . . . now take six weeks to reach the Pacific, instead of **the normal one week,** by which time most of them die. (BNC, J32 140)

(54)   She learned with sadness in her heart that **their recent one night of love** had been after he had met a young Vietnamese man . . . (BNC, CEC 2013)

Conditions on Noun Ellipsis in English 63

(55) Shifting the work across by **that critical one needle position** is child's play, . . . (BNC, CGX 1533)

(56) Because you could I mean you could do **the empty one tin** in a day really. (BNC, HES 43)

(57) Oh hang on that's **the wrong one hand** on . . . (BNC, HV0 1253)

(58) Yeah and that was **the only one night** we never took the video camera with us . . . (BNC, KCP 4848)

(59) Look at **this just one rose**. (BNC, KCV 4181)

(60) . . . **the initial one sale a year** was extended into two annual sales in each category. (BNC, EBS 2162)

These data show that *one* as numeral can follow prenominal adjectives. Therefore, Dahl's argument against the numeral status of stressed *one* has to be discarded, but the second point she puts forth is more severe. Dahl observes that the plural form of *one* can be stressed as well. As numeral *one* does not inflect, the use of *one* in the following example is clearly anaphoric.

(61) Those pictures are my favorite ONES. (Dahl 1985: 31)

I do not have a definite answer to this. I suspect that adjectives constitute a different case because they allow for both stressed and unstressed *one*. *Every*, however, only takes the stressed version. In addition, it never takes a plural noun. The parallels between the use of numerals and the use of *one* with *every* attested in the BNC data are a robust indication for the numeral status of *one*.

Adjectives that allow for stressed *one* are a very interesting matter, as many of them also allow for noun ellipsis, such as ordinals and superlatives.[11] This aspect requires further investigation.

4.2.3 Some Remarks on the Definite Article

The definite article does not allow for noun ellipsis, which ties in with the claims made above. It is compatible with a count and a mass reading, and hence is unspecified in terms of countability. Allan (1980: 543) provides the following example to illustrate that both mass (*the lightning*) and count structures (*the car*) display the definite article.[12]

(62) The lightning has frightened Caspar, and he's hiding under the car.

Furthermore, the definite article does not add any restrictive information about the entity in question. Thus, it does not satisfy the contrast condition. This, however, wrongly predicts that *one* should not be licit with the definite article either. But again, this problem is more apparent than real, and an

64 *The Elliptical Noun Phrase in English*

explanation can be sought along the lines of the analysis of *every*. First, the defining properties needed for the use of *one* can occur as post-modifying clauses (finite, example 63, and non-finite, example 64) as well as prepositional phrases (example 65):

(63) Even better, go down to your local computer shop and ask them to show you several different ways to back up, then choose **the one which seems easiest.** (BNC, A0C 674)

(64) However, Mr. Wilson said that other Scottish bridges, like **the one being built at Dornoch,** had been publicly funded. (BNC, A1Y 66)

(65) In the summer his vegetable garden is as neat and attractive as **the one at Villandry.** (BNC, A0D 2600)

A possible explanation is offered in Dahl (1985), where the definite article is listed as an element that does not allow for *one*-anaphora except for the use with post-modifiers; only unstressed *one* is licit here. But instances of *one* without any post-modificational elements can be found.

(66) At this point it is necessary to distinguish between foot sweeps and hooks. In fact, there isn't a great deal of difference between the two and **the one** merges into the other. (BNC, A0M 1056,7)

(67) They are pieces of writing which are distinct in law; the author of **the one** could not be sued for the other, or for collaborating in it. (BNC, A05 1148)

(68) If anyone can be said to deserve a holiday, she told herself firmly, then I am **the one.** (BNC, AD1 3215)

(69) With a spicy noggin to follow—but just **the one!** (BNC, AR7 356)

(70) Once, in the distance, he saw a girl who might have been **the one.** (BNC, ASN 1568)

(71) I went through a bunch of necks and felt them, and after feeling about twenty I said to the guy, "This is **the one.** I want you to take this neck and make it a neck-through-body Strat-style guitar." (BNC, C9N 219,20)

Dahl suggests that *one* is made licit "by either the discourse environment [. . .] or by the general situation" (1985: 12), which is apparent in the following examples:

(72) A: Do you know the man I'm talking about?

B: Yes, I know the one (you're talking about).

Conditions on Noun Ellipsis in English 65

(73) Nixon's the one.

Dahl concludes that here "the contexts permits an interpretation with modifiers" (1985: 12).

Rather than treating *the one* as a special case of *one*-insertion, *one* should be analyzed as a numeral in these cases, along the lines of *every one*. The claim can be motivated as follows. First, the above examples display contexts where singularity of an item is stressed. In example (66) there are two hooks and one of them merges into the other one. The same applies to example (67). In examples (68) and (69), it is also evident that the sets under discussion only contain one member each, that is, there is only one person who deserves going on vacation and there is only one spicy noggin to be consumed, emphasized by the use of *just*. In example (71), there are a range of necks but the speaker only wants one of them. In terms of example (70), more context is needed:

(74) He could not say what he intended to do if he found <u>the girl</u> (1566). After all, conversation with her would be limited and he could hardly hope to find out if her injury was real or not, short of tearing the bandage from her leg (1567). Once, in the distance, he saw a girl who might have been **the one** (1568). (BNC, ASN)

In this context, there is one particular referent again—one girl the speaker is looking for—indicated by the use of the definite article in line 1566.

The examples demonstrate that there is a proper context to emphasize singularity; hence, *one* is used as a stressed form to signal uniqueness.

Dahl argues against treating *one* as a numeral, because plural *ones* can be stressed as well, when it follows certain adjectives and, hence, the stressed version of *one* cannot be a numeral. As mentioned, this is a severe problem. I do not have a definite answer to this, but I assume that the use of plural *ones* is even more restricted in these syntactic environments. A BNC search for *the one* and *the ones* followed by a finite verb or a punctuation mark (to exclude prepositions, relative pronouns, and nonfinite clauses) gives 543 hits for *the one* without post-modifier, some of which were presented above, and only 23 hits for *the ones*.[13] Interestingly, many of the latter hits contain post-modifiers, which do not immediately follow *one*, that is, we are dealing with discontinuous noun phrases.

(75) They are **the ones**, too, who celebrate a birth. (BNC, A6V 142)

(76) Oh yes, yes, cos they're **the ones**, they're, they're **the ones who wanted to, to camp** (BNC, KDR 865)

Some of the few true instances are provided below.

(77) Free men on the frontiers of industry, shocking the respectable of all classes, the heroes of an unofficial folklore of masculinity, they played

66 *The Elliptical Noun Phrase in English*

the same sort of role as sailors and frontier miners and prospectors, though earning more than **the ones,** and lacking the others' hope of making their fortune. (BNC, J0P 435)

(78) What about a fried egg sandwich they're **the ones!** (BNC, KDM 14244)

(79) These are **the ones.** (BNC, KDP 765)

To sum up, the data from the BNC suggest that the use of plural *ones* with a definite article is marginal whereas the singular is much more frequent. Although this does not prove that *one* following a definite article without further modifiers is a numeral (which then precedes a silent empty noun), it indicates that the idea of not treating this use of *one* as the anaphoric form might be on the right track. I leave this open for future research.

4.3 THE STRUCTURE OF THE ELLIPTICAL NOUN PHRASE

It has been illustrated that elements that allow for noun ellipsis have to indicate countability and that they have to dominate the ellipsis site immediately (see Section 4.1.1)—unspecified elements such as property-denoting adjectives do not allow for a silent noun. This raises the question why [± count] has to be on the rightmost, or in other words, the most deeply embedded prenominal overt element in the noun phrase.

In the literature, however, although being noticed, the requirement has been merely accepted as a fact, but generally not much further explanation has been sought (but see Corver & van Koppen 2011, whose proposal will be partly adopted). Llombart-Huesca (2002), for example, claims, "if an adjective is present between the element with the strong agreement features and the empty $Number^0$, licensing is blocked" (example 78). But this constraint does not naturally follow from licensing. Agreement relations, for example, generally hold if further material intervenes, even across longer distances. Llombart-Huesca (2002: 78n10) makes reference to the head movement constraint (HMC, see Travis 1984), according to which head movement must not skip intervening head positions. The structure she proposes for the nominal domain is as follows:

(80) a. many lazy ones

b. $[_{QP} [_{Q0} \text{many}] [_{AP} \text{lazy} [_{NumP} [_{Num0} \text{ones}] [_{NP} \emptyset]]]]$

Without going into detail here, a short remark is in order. The HMC applies if there are intervening heads. This implies that the intervening adjectives, which block the licensing mechanism, would have to be heads. However, it is commonly accepted that an attributive adjective heads an AP that

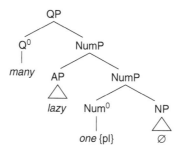

Figure 4.1 Structural representation of *many lazy ones*

is adjoined to NP (or NumP) (see, e.g., Svenonius 1994). A modified version of the structure proposed by Llombart-Huesca is provided in Figure 4.1.

Thus, there are no heads but phrases that intervene. Hence, the HMC does not apply and an explanation for this matter has to be sought along different lines. The question closely relates to how the ellipsis site is construed. Analyses of ellipsis can be divided into accounts which assume that the ellipsis site contains some kind of structure and those that consider the missing material is not syntactically represented in any way.[14] As argued in Section 3.1, in the present approach noun ellipsis is considered to involve a silent nominal element; thus, strictly speaking, noun ellipsis, as understood here, is not an instance of phonological deletion of lexical material, but, rather, *one* is deleted (see Ross 1969). In order to show to the merits of such an approach, I will briefly discuss alternative accounts for ellipsis in the nominal domain.

A nonstructural approach—as the name suggests—assumes that there is no structure within the ellipsis site. To my knowledge there are no recent nonstructural accounts for ellipsis in the nominal domain. More traditional approaches to grammar suggest that noun ellipsis cases are instances of adjective-to-noun or determiner-to-noun conversion. Halliday and Hasan, for example, claim that "an elliptical item is one which, as it were, leaves specific structural slots to be filled from elsewhere" (1976: 143). They assume the nominal group to comprise the following positions:

(81) those   two   fast   electric   trains   with pantographs
     Deictic Numerative Epithet Classifier   Head   Qualifier

A further assumption is that the head is an obligatory position to be filled:

[t]he function of Head, which is always filled, is normally served by the common noun, proper noun or pronoun expressing the Thing. [. . .] Now under certain circumstances the common noun may be omitted and the function of Head taken on by one of these other elements. This is what is meant by nominal ellipsis. (Halliday & Hasan 1976: 147).

68   *The Elliptical Noun Phrase in English*

Although they do not explicitly mention conversion, Halliday and Hasan speak of an "upgrading of a word," which necessarily involves a categorical shift. Another possible realization of a nonstructural approach could take the nominal head to be absent from the structure.

Both ideas are problematic for various reasons. First, the latter possible scenario clearly has to be rejected, because if a nominal head was missing, it would be unclear why the elliptical phrase occurs in syntactic positions typical of noun phrases.

The weaknesses of a conversion approach are less obvious. If the last of the remnants in the following examples were considered nouns, this would have an apparent advantage: It could explain why countability needs to be expressed on the element immediately dominating the ellipsis site because this would simply parallel the expression of number on the head noun.

(82) a. If you wait to be assured of winning every contest, you will win **very few.** (COCA, 2004 SPOK)

   b. Beats one man, then **another** and then **a third.** (BNC, K4T)

This could also account for the unacceptability of *one*-insertion with numerals and the like. If these determiners and adjectives are nouns (or pronouns), it naturally follows that a further nominal element is blocked in that position. However, with some elements the use of *one* is optional. An approach such as the one discussed above entails that a noun phrase such as *a third* is fundamentally different from *a third one* with respect to its structural properties. From a theoretical perspective, this is less desirable because it overlooks the parallels between the two.

While the latter aspect could somehow be resolved in certain frameworks, the use of adverbial modifiers poses additional problems. Consider the following examples:

(83) Among the first to exploit this property on an industrial scale in the eighteenth century were William Worthington and William Bass, and when trademarks began to be registered under the Trade Marks Act of 1875, **the very first** was William Bass's familiar red triangle. (BNC, B0A 480)

(84) Then, when he comes to give examples of "the multiplicity of language-games," **the very first** is giving orders, and obeying them. (BNC, CK1 1354)

Here the intensifying adverb *very* indicates that a reanalysis of these elements as nouns is somewhat dubious.[15]

This brief discussion has illustrated, I hope, that a nonstructural approach is less desirable for noun ellipsis (see Olsen 1987 for a detailed analysis of the adjectival status of the remnant elements).

Structural approaches can be roughly divided into those assuming null lexical elements to be involved (such as null anaphora *pro*, see, e.g. Lobeck 1995, 2006) and those that take syntactic structure to be fully represented in the ellipsis site and to be deleted only phonologically. Such a PF-deletion approach (see, e.g., Merchant 2001) is based on the assumption that the ellipsis site contains the same syntax as the nonelliptical counterpart. However, this is incompatible with the assumption that both *one* and the element in elliptical noun phrases are descriptively empty nouns, that is, N^0-elements, which underlies the present analysis, because it cannot handle the obvious parallels.[16] A way out of this is to assume that *one* requires obligatory PF-deletion of the nominal, as has been suggested by Alexiadou and Gengel (forthcoming). But this presupposes that *one* takes NP as a complement—Alexiadou and Gengel consider *one* to be inserted into a projection (classifier phrase) dominating NP—and hence cannot be a noun.

Licensing and identification of an empty pronominal as an approach to noun ellipsis is problematic for a number of reasons. First, because *one* and the silent noun are not in complementary distribution, *one* cannot be some kind of last resort strategy that applies when the licensing of the empty element fails. Second, such an account does not acknowledge that *one* is also subject to constraints—the contrast condition. What is more, it cannot account for the peculiar behavior of adjectives as interveners. There is nothing in the nature of adjectives that would predict this kind of effect—they should not be able to block a syntactic mechanism. The most interesting fact is certainly that linear order rather than hierarchical structure seems to be the crucial factor. The features that formally license an empty element should not be affected by linear order.

As will become clear, linear order and adjacency are the relevant factors. Most of the above issues can be circumvented if the focus is shifted from the licensing of noun ellipsis to the question of why *one* cannot be used in certain contexts.

4.3.1 Deletion Under Adjacency

Even though the relevance of linear order is gaining more ground in the discussion of certain syntactic phenomena (see, e.g., Neeleman & van de Koot 2006; Richards 2010 and references therein), the aspect of adjectives blocking the licensing of noun ellipsis has not received much attention. Interestingly, there are further instances of a similar adjectival behavior. In Swedish, for example, an effect called double definiteness (or determiner spreading, see Alexiadou et al. 2007) can be witnessed. Definiteness is always marked on the noun in the form of a suffix (examples from Embick & Noyer 2001; see also Heck et al. 2008):

(85) mus-en
    mouse-DEF
    "the mouse"

70   *The Elliptical Noun Phrase in English*

However, when an adjectival modifier intervenes, an additional marker of definiteness occurs.

(86) a. *gamla mus-en
        old mouse-DEF

     b. den gamla mus-en
        the old mouse-DEF
        "the old mouse"

In this case, adjectives display the same intervention effect as in the case of noun ellipsis. Another instance of this phenomenon can be found in Dutch. In the following examples, numeral *éen* ("one") and the indefinite article cannot be adjacent.

(87) a. *éen 'n rare

     b. *one a strange
        (Barbiers 2005: 171)

Again, an intervening element licenses the simultaneous use of both elements:

(88) a. éen zo 'n boek

     b. one such (a) book
        (ibid.)

Barbiers proposes the following analysis: *Éen* is specified for [indefinite] [singular] [focus], and *'n* is endowed with the features [indefinite] and [singular]. As the features on *'n* are redundant, the latter is phonologically deleted. The rule he suggests says "[l]eave D empty at PF when D and Num are adjacent and the features of D are a subset of the features of Num" (Barbiers 2005: 172).[17] This is considered an instance of syntactic haplology.

Prima facie, such a rule may sound dubious because haplology usually presupposes phonological similarity or even identity. But as Neeleman and van de Koot (2006) argue, a number of deletion phenomena can best be accounted for in terms of avoidance repetition of identical syntactic features. They state that:

> [g]iven that the spell-out rules relate morpho-syntactic objects to their phonological form, one would expect to find cases in which deletion or suppletion is triggered by syntactic features even though the morphemes affected are not phonologically identical in isolation. (Neeleman & van de Koot 2006: 700)

Conditions on Noun Ellipsis in English 71

If a functional element carries features that are a subset of the features expressed on the adjacent element, it can be deleted. To what extent this applies is language and construction-specific.

It was argued above that a deletion mechanism that applies at the surface is more desirable, as it circumvents the aforementioned problems, that is, the unexpected role of adjectives as interveners that does not follow from their structural properties. As Barbiers suggests, deletion under adjacency might also be applicable to other syntactic categories. Noun ellipsis might hence be analyzed as follows: a cardinal numeral (>1), for example, is an element that expresses countability and plurality. *Ones* also expresses countability and plurality. Being devoid of descriptive content, it adds no further information, that is, its features are an improper subset of those expressed on the element that is adjacent to it. Thus, it is deleted. If an adjective intervenes, the deletion rule does not apply anymore, because the two elements expressing the same features are not adjacent. This means that noun ellipsis with, for example, numerals contains the noun *one* as well, but this noun is deleted under adjacency (see also Kester's 1996b claim that *one* is superfluous in these contexts). In the same vein, singular *one* can be deleted if it is preceded by an adjacent [+count] element.[18]

The rules can be formulated as follows:

(89) Deletion under adjacency I

Delete *one* if the adjacent element preceding it is [+plural].[19]

(90) Deletion under adjacency II

Optionally delete one if the adjacent element preceding it is [+count].

The question remains why deletion is optional here while at the same time it seems to be obligatory with plural elements.[20] Presumably, this has to do with the fact that elements like the ordinals do not necessarily take singular nouns, as pointed out before.

(91) Inspect plants regularly and spray at **the first signs** of attack. (= example 20) (BNC, A0G)

As antecedent and elliptical noun phrase do not always match in number, *one* could be used in these contexts to disambiguate number.[21] In example (92), for instance, it is not clear whether the elliptical noun phrase is singular or plural:

(92) But there was absolutely nothing of the girl herself in the letters nor of the woman she became between <u>the first letters</u> and **the last**. (COCA, 2003 FIC)

72 *The Elliptical Noun Phrase in English*

However, this does not explain why *one* should be allowed with *another* and *each*, which are clearly singular elements. A further conceivable reason could be that plural, in contrast to singular, is overtly marked and that the overt expression of redundant features is not tolerated.[22]

A further aspect to be addressed is noun ellipsis with mass interpretations, that is, phrases where *one* cannot be used. The deletion mechanism works in a similar way: If an adjacent quantifier is specified for [-count], the empty noun remains silent.

(93) and then the people run out of <u>water</u>. They find **some**, but it is not fit to drink. (BNC, ACG)

If an adjective intervenes and blocks adjacency, the noun has to become overt in analogy to the mechanism described above. However, because the English language does not provide a phonetic form for the empty noun in mass contexts, the only way to use an overt form is to repeat the lexical noun.[23]

Evidence for an empty noun in a noncount context can be derived from the Abstract Construction outlined in Chapter 1. It was pointed out that a definite article and a descriptive adjective without an antecedent result in two possible readings—generic reference to humans with a certain property or reference to something abstract.

(94) a. The rich cannot enter the kingdom of Heaven. (= example 5, Chapter 1) (Payne & Huddleston 2002: 411)

    b. This is verging on the immoral. (ibid.)

In example (94b), a mass reading emerges. Hence, the empty noun must be compatible with mass readings (see also Kester 1996b; Panagiotidis 2003a), which supports the claim that there is a silent noun in mass contexts as well. For reasons to be laid out in detail in what follows, I assume that the empty noun is spelled out as *one* as soon as it combines with number—an option that is not available in mass contexts.

4.3.2 Nominal Classification and Ellipsis

The above suggestions are fully compatible with a traditional approach to countability where a specification for count or mass is contained in the lexical entries of the nouns. This view implies that there are two empty nouns: One of them is a mass noun that always remains silent, and the other, *one*, is a count noun that has a phonological form but is deleted under certain circumstances. However, as pointed out in Chapter 3, in more recent approaches to noun ellipsis, reference is made to nominal classification, which means that parallels are drawn between English and classifier languages.

Conditions on Noun Ellipsis in English 73

Nominal anaphora in those languages indeed suggests a close link between noun ellipsis and classification, because classifiers are used anaphorically. As Ngyuen (1957: 130) points out, in Vietnamese, "[t]he classifier may also be used as a substitute when the antecedent has already been sufficiently identified by the previous context."

(95) a. Tôi có ba con mèo, hai con trắng, một con den
I have three CL cat two CL white one CL black
"I have three cats two white and one black."

b. Bà mu?n mua mây qua? –Ba qua.
how many? want buy you CL three CL

How many (fruits) do you want to buy?—Three.
(Nguyen Dinh Hoa 1957: 130, gloss added)

The example illustrates that the elliptical noun phrase contains a classifier in addition to the modifier(s) expressing a new property or quantity. In example (95a), the antecedent noun, *mèo* "cat," is accompanied by the classifier for living things, *con*, in order to be quantifiable by the numeral *ba* "three." The two subsequent NPs, *hai con trắng* "'two white ones" and *một con den* "one black one," are elliptical—they contain a numeral, *hai* "two" and *một* "one," and a modifying adjective, *trắng* "white" and *den* "black," but they lack the head noun *mèo*. The classifier is present in the elliptical phrase as well. Similarly, the classifier for fruits *qua* is repeated in the elliptical phrase in example (95b). This is attested for other classifier languages as well; see Downing (1986) for Japanese, Conklin (1981) for Thai, and Saito et al. (2008) for Chinese.

4.3.2.1 Different Nominal Classification Systems

Obviously, there is a close connection between nominal classification and noun ellipsis, which also became evident in the above discussion of the relevance of the mass-count distinction for elliptical noun phrases in English. However, English is not a classifier language and the languages differ in how the mass-count distinction is drawn. Consider the following data from Mandarin Chinese, a classifier language:

(96) a. san ping jiu
three bottle liquor
"three bottles of liquor"

b. san ba mi
three handful rice
"three handfuls of rice"

74 *The Elliptical Noun Phrase in English*

    c. san   wan   tang
       three bowl   soup
       "three bowls of soup"
       (Cheng & Sybesma 1999: 514)

Chinese creates countable measure units by making use of measure phrases (this is why Cheng and Sybesma call this type of element "massifier").[24] A similar mechanism is available in English as well.

(97) a. a bottle/glass of wine

    b. three grains/bowls of rice

What sets Chinese apart from English is the need for a classifier with what corresponds to a count noun in English, as the following examples (taken from Cheng & Sybesma 1999) make clear.

(98) a. san   ge   ren
      three CL   people
      "three persons"
    b. san   zhi bi
      three CL   pen
      "three pens"
    c. san   ben shu
      three CL   book
      "three books"

Both types of classifier are subsumed under the term "numeral classifier" (for a disambiguation of the term "classifier," see Grinevald 2000) because they are used in quantifying contexts. This kind of classifier can be divided into two semantic subtypes (ibid.), the "sortal classifier," which categorizes by an inherent property of the referent, and the "mensural classifier," which identifies countable units. Whereas a language such as English (and German) has the latter type, the former is considered to be exclusive to numeral classifier languages, the "paradigm type" (Allan 1977: 286) of classifier languages. This shows that language has several nominal categories and categorization mechanisms at its disposal. There are different nominal classification systems ranging from lexical class terms over numeral classifiers in the so-called classifier languages to grammatical systems of nominal classification such as gender (see, e.g., Grinevald 2000).

4.3.2.2 Noun Ellipsis and the Mass-Count Distinction in English

As English has lost its grammatical gender system, the only category that is grammatically marked on nouns in Present Day English is number. Bouchard

Conditions on Noun Ellipsis in English   75

(2002) argues that number serves an individuation function (see Section 4.2), it distinguishes mass and count. An illustrative example is presented by de Belder (2011: 177).

(99) a. I tasted chocolate.

   b. I tasted chocolates.

In example (99a), *chocolate* denotes an uncountable substance. Adding plural morphology results in a count reading. The noun phrase in example (99b) is either interpreted as referring to different kinds of chocolate or to several units or pieces of chocolate (de Belder 2011); the mass reading, however, is blocked. As number morphology is incompatible with mass interpretations, some researchers propose that it is the counterpart of numeral classifiers (see Borer 2005, de Belder 2011)—a view that ties in with the general observation that languages either have number morphology or numeral classifiers (see Svenonius 2008)—which has some further implications concerning the structure of the noun phrase.[25] Borer (2005), who presents an elaborate account for the mass-count distinction, suggests that noun phrases denoting countable entities differ structurally from mass-denoting ones. This naturally follows if number is taken to reside on a separate functional head, as proposed by Ritter (1991)—mass nouns cannot be pluralized, which suggests that there is no number (or classifier) projection available. Borer further argues that this structural distinction makes a lexical specification for mass and count redundant: as syntax determines whether something receives a count interpretation or—in the absence of the dividing element—a mass reading, nouns are unmarked with respect to countability.[26] This entails that countability is a property of the noun phrase rather than the noun (see also Allan 1980).

This rather brief summary illustrates the aspects relevant for the current proposal. I adopt the idea that mass and count denoting noun phrases differ structurally in that number is not available in the former. The question whether this necessarily implies that the mass-count distinction is only structurally determined, and not lexically encoded, is of minor importance for the present work and is left open.

The proposal is as follows. Elliptical noun phrases contain an anaphoric N^0 element. This element is not just semantically empty, it also does not have a phonological form. If the anaphoric phrase denotes a mass, the element remains silent in N^0. If the phrase denotes a countable entity, a number projection (referred to as classifier phrase in other approaches) dominating NP is available. As soon as the empty noun combines with number morphology, it is spelled out as *one* (or *ones*), unless, of course, it is deleted under the aforementioned adjacency requirement. In other words, noun ellipsis implies the deletion of *one* (see Ross 1967), at least in count noun phrases. Considerable variation even in those cases that are classified as contexts that only allow for *one* (see Stirling & Huddleston 2002) suggests that the choice between *one* and a silent noun is made at the surface.

76 *The Elliptical Noun Phrase in English*

This proposal has several advantages. First, it is fully compatible with the assumption that *one* is the overt version of a silent empty noun. Thus, it captures the parallels between the two empty elements laid out in detail in Section 3.1. It also explains why *one* can only be used in countable noun phrases. Furthermore, the parallels between English and classifier languages are taken into account: As pointed out above, in the latter, classifiers are required as remnants in elliptical noun phrases.

4.3.2.3 Non–Antecedent-Based Uses of Empty Nouns

Further support for noun ellipsis being related to nominal classification can be derived from the non–antecedent-based uses of nounless noun phrases, the Human Construction and the Abstract Construction.

These constructions have the rather fixed form definite article + adjective.[27] The Human Construction is a countable noun phrase: Verb agreement indicates plurality, even though the construction itself does not contain overt number marking.

(100) **The poor** are collectively starved of political resources and support. (BNC, EG0 263)

As already mentioned in Chapter 1, the phrase receives a generic interpretation (see, e.g., Quirk et al. 1985; Payne & Huddleston 2002) and denotes an entire category of human beings characterized by some defining property expressed by the adjective. Reference to individuals is not possible, in contrast to German, where the construction readily allows for individual reference.[28]

(101) Ich war **der Dicke** und so habe ich angefangen zu spielen.
I   was the fat   and so have I   started   to play

"I was the fat one/guy and thus I started playing."
(DPA09/MAI.03357)

(102) Wollen Sie   künftig von **einem Dicken** regiert werden oder von
want   you   in the of a   fat   reigned be.FUT or   of
future

einem Dürren?
a   gaunt

"Do you want to be reigned by a fat guy or a gaunt one in the future?"
(B98/FEB.08964)

Even though the Human Construction generally occurs without a nominal head, there are parallels to *one*-insertion strategies. The following example

Conditions on Noun Ellipsis in English   77

from Stirling and Huddleston (2002: 1516) shows that *one* also receives a [+human] interpretation when it is not bound by an antecedent.

(103) Kim's not the **one responsible for the delay.**

There are further uses of *one* that parallel the Human Construction. The noun phrases in the examples below denote human beings defined by a property expressed through an adjectival modifier.

(104) Both Ipa and Xucate had become ill then but had survived. Sometimes entire villages perished. Those who lived never got the sickness again and were forced to wait on **the sick ones** and bury the dead. (COCA, 1995 FIC)

(105) Last night, perhaps, the bombs that fell from Rob's plane had killed women and children and old, helpless men, but for all that he was a tender lover. She wished **the dead ones** could have known that. (= example 15, Chapter 3) (BNC, CEH 489–90)

In these cases, the phrases are not used generically. Rather, they refer to subgroups of sick people—those who suffer from a particular disease, "the sickness." This differs from the generic use of *the sick* in the following example:

(106) . . . the sort of people that walk into hospitals and start praying for **the sick** to be healed. (BNC, KPV 3247)

Similarly, in example (105) the phrase *the dead ones* refers to the people who died under particular circumstances (the bombing by Rob) and not to the entire class of dead people. Furthermore, even indefinite singular reference is possible with adjectives and the use of *one*:

(107) . . . the "human organ" in the cooler box, on its way to **some poor one** strapped in a hospital bed. (= example 16, Chapter 3) (COCA, 2001 FIC)

Obviously, the use of *one* and hence the overt expression of number in these examples brings about nongeneric reference. This ties in nicely with Cheng and Sybesma's (1999) claim that in classifier languages, a noun plus classifier combination cannot receive a generic interpretation.[29] Number, hosted on the empty noun *one* has a classification effect; it signals that the denotation of the noun phrase is countable, number being incompatible with denotation of masses. This may seem to predict that number blocks genericity, which certainly is not the case, because

78 *The Elliptical Noun Phrase in English*

bare plurals commonly allow for generic reference (see, e.g. Krifka et al. 1995). The noun phrases under consideration here, however, differ in that they are plural and definite. Definite plurals, with minor exceptions, usually do not permit generic interpretations.[30] According to Lyons (1991: 112) the noun phrase *the miners* in the following examples can only be understood as nongeneric.

(108) a. The miners really earn what they get.

b. Harry has no sympathy for the miners.

This is in line with Payne and Huddleston's (2002) claim that if *people* is added to the Human Construction, the noun phrase loses its generic reading.[31]

To sum up, the Human Construction differs from ordinary generic noun phrases in that it is a definite plural. An additional *one* or *ones* allows for nongeneric reference, which suggests that *one*, or strictly speaking the number specification it bears, has a function parallel to that of numeral classifiers that preclude a generic reading.[32] This provides further support for a classification-based approach to noun ellipsis.

In this context, the role of inflection in the noun phrase and its impact on the licensing of noun ellipsis become evident. Number is the only category morphologically expressed on English (count) nouns. When no noun is present to host number morphology, the empty noun takes on this function and is spelled out as *one(s)*. Due to number being a property of count structures, the empty noun can only become overt in the latter. This implies, in contrast to, for example, Bouchard (2002), who also relates the restrictions on noun ellipsis in English to the need to code number on N, that *one* is always present in elliptical count noun phrases. However, if an adjacent element already marks the noun phrase as countable, *one* is not required and can be deleted. An intervening adjective makes *one* "visible." Thus, the impoverished inflectional system of the English language is responsible for the rather strict conditions on noun ellipsis in English, as has been proposed by Lobeck (1995) and others. This also explains why there are fewer constraints on elliptical noun phrases in German, which has a richer inflectional system, encoding case, number, and gender in the nominal domain. An integration of this idea into the above ideas is developed in what follows.

4.3.2.4 Noun Ellipsis in German

As illustrated in Section 2.2, in order to license noun ellipsis an element needs inflection.[33] This becomes evident in the (rare) cases of elements that do not inflect in prenominal position, such as the adjectives *lila* "purple,", *rosa* "pink," which are substituted by inflecting nonstandard versions or compounds in elliptical noun phrases.

Conditions on Noun Ellipsis in English   79

(109)

An	einem	besonderen	Tag	wie	an	Weihnachten oder	Ostern trägt man
on	a	special	day	like	on	Christmas or	Easter wears one
als	Pfarrer	ein	weißes	Messgewand,	an	normalen	
as	priest	a	white	liturgical garment.	on	ordinary	
				ACC.NEUT.SG			

Tagen	ein	**grünes,**	in	der	Fastenzeit ein	lilanes,
days	a	green.ACC.	in	the	lent a	purple.ACC.
		NEUT.SG				NEUT.SG

| am | Karfreitag | ein | **rotes.** |
| on the | Good Friday | a | red.ACC.NEUT.SG |

"On a special day such as Christmas or Easter priests wear a white liturgical garment, on ordinary days a green one, during lent a purple one and on Good Friday a red one." (= example 29, Chapter 2)
(8M07/APR.02637)

(110)

Der	rote	<u>Umschlag</u>		muss in den **lilafarbenen**
The	red	envelope.NOM.MASC.SG		must in the purple-colored.ACC.MASC.SG
gesteckt	werden.			
put	be.			

"The red envelope has to be put into the purple one." (= example 30, Chapter 2)
(Z07/FEB.00438)

Furthermore, there are elements that have special forms for the use in elliptical noun phrases. Indefinite elements such as the indefinite article *ein*, *kein* "no," and the possessives display suffixes for singular nominative masculine and neuter as well as singular accusative neuter, only when they are not followed by a noun.[34]

(111)

Aber	in	der	Garderobe	war	kein	<u>Bild</u>		von	ihrem
but	in	the	checkroom	was	no	picture.NOM.NEUT.SG		of	her
Mann	und	auch	**keines**	von	dem	Kind.			
husband and		also	no.NOM.NEUT.SG	of	the	child			

"But in the checkroom there was no picture of her husband and none of the child either." (= example 26, Chapter 2)
(HMP09/MAR.00847)

In light of the above-developed account, the question arises which categories need to be expressed in German noun phrases. Lobeck (1995) proposes different sets of features that license ellipsis (*pro* in her approach, see Section 3.2.1) such as a [+Case, +Gender] on singular adjectives and [+ Case, +Gender, +Partitive] on the singular numeral and quantifier.[35] However, this rather complex feature specification for German [Case, Number,

80 *The Elliptical Noun Phrase in English*

Gender, Partitivity] can be collapsed into a more concise requirement, in analogy to what has been done for English.[36] First, partitivity is ruled out for the reasons given in Section 3.3.2; suffice it to say at this point that it remains entirely unclear in how far partitivity can be considered an agreement feature in German. The remaining features certainly are attested in the German noun phrase, where agreement obtains in case, number, and gender. But it will be argued that they are not of equal importance for noun ellipsis. Rather, the crucial feature is gender, for reasons to be outlined in what follows.

Interesting insights come from elements that lack suffixes for nominative masculine and neuter as well as accusative neuter. Example (111) illustrates that *kein* bears the suffix *-es* in nominative neuter elliptical noun phrases. The same suffix is used for the accusative in example (112), the masculine form is *-er* in example (113).

(112)

Um	ein	Darlehen	zu bekommen, muß man erst beweisen,
to	a	loan ACC.NEUT.SG	to obtain must one first prove that
man	**keines**	braucht.	
one	no.acc.neut.sg	need	

"In order to obtain a loan, one has to prove first that one needs none."
(WPD/MMM.11234)

(113)

Das	Chamäleon	besteht	aus	einer	Gruppe	von	Sternen,	von
the	Chameleon	consist	of	a	group	of	star.DAT.MASC.PL	of
denen	**keiner**	die	4.	Größenklasse	überschreitet.			
those	no.NOM.MASC.SG	the	4th	stellar magnitude	exceed			

"The Chameleon comprises a group of stars none of which exceeds the fourth stellar magnitude."
(WPD/CCC.02336)

Due to the syncretism of the two suffixes for neuter, only gender is distinguished, which suggests that gender is the crucial feature in these contexts. This idea receives support from the works of various authors who relate the licensing of noun ellipsis to gender (cf. e.g. Barbiers 2005 on Dutch, and Bernstein 1993 on noun ellipsis in Romance). Most interesting for the present approach is a connection to nominal classification and its interaction with noun ellipsis (cf. Alexiadou & Gengel forthcoming), which will be made explicit in what follows.[37]

In Section 4.3.2.1, it was mentioned that languages have very different classifier systems. Their categorization has received a fair amount of attention in the literature (see, e.g., Allan 1977, Croft 1994, Grinevald 2000, Senft 2000). Gender is typically categorized as a noun class system, which differs from numeral classification in various aspects, the most important of which for the present analysis being that all nouns of a language are classified and that gender is realized in agreement patterns. Furthermore, there is no immediate relation between gender and the mass-count distinction. But as different as classifier systems may be, they share a common function, as Greenberg (1978: 78) argues: "[it] is that nouns are continuing discourse subjects and therefore in constant need of referential devices of identification [. . .] classification is a help in narrowing the range of possible identification." This also becomes apparent in anaphoric contexts, where classifiers are used as reference tracking devices. The latter also turns out to be, according to Corbett (1991: 322), "the major function of gender" (see also Croft 1994 on the semantic/pragmatic function of determination (reference) of noun classes). This suggests that it is, in fact, gender that needs to be expressed in the German noun phrase, even when there is no lexical noun. Further evidence for this derives from the Human Construction. As pointed out in 4.3.2.3, German readily allows for the Human Construction to be used nongenerically. Even singular reference is possible, whereby the referent is unambiguously marked as male or female human being. Similarly, other languages with gender systems such as Dutch and French allow for (nongeneric) singular reference (Kester 1996a, Sleeman 1996). In English, this is only licit if number is overtly expressed through *one*.

With gender being established as the morphosyntactic licensing condition on noun ellipsis in German, the status of the inflectional suffixes that only show up with ellipsis as well as the nature of the silent noun need closer scrutiny. Particularly, the distribution of these suffixes sheds light on the matter—if *kein* is followed by an adjective, it remains uninflected (provided it is nom. masculine or nom./acc. neuter).

(114)

Das war auch ein <u>Gespenst,</u> aber nur **ein ganz kleines.**
That was also a   ghost   but only a   very small.NOM.NEUT.SG
"That was a ghost, too, but only a very small one."
(HAZ08/SEP.05408)

Similarly, noninflecting adjectives can occur in elliptical noun phrases provided that the rightmost element in the prenominal string bears an inflectional ending. This became evident in example (38) in Chapter 2, repeated below.

(115) Neben den von Andreina Ertico in Wolfsburg erstandenen <u>Siegerschuhen</u> gefielen Linna Hensel ganz besonders auffallend grünfarbene, moderne schwarze und sexy **lila glitzernde.** (= example 38, Chapter 2)

(BRZ08/MAI.16014)

There are two important implications of this observation. First, adjacency also seems to be crucial in German. Second, the inflectional ending that only occurs in elliptical contexts resembles English *one*, as has been

82 *The Elliptical Noun Phrase in English*

argued for dialects of Dutch by Corver and van Koppen (2011). The basic ideas of their account will be adopted in what follows.

Corver and van Koppen assume that there are two noun ellipsis strategies available: "pronominalization," that is, an overt form such as *one*, and "elision," a silent form. Based on data from Dutch varieties, which also display the requirement for the licensor to be on the rightmost prenominal element, they argue for an analysis of the apparent inflectional endings as weak pronouns. In Afrikaans, for example, the suffix *-e* can only occur once in the string preceding the ellipsis site.

(116) Jan het ['n groot wit konyn] gekoop . . .
Jan has a white rabbit bought . . .

"Jan has bought a white rabbit."

a. en Piet het ['n groot swarte] gekoop.
and Piet has a big black-e bought.

"and Piet bought a big black one."

b. *en Piet het ['n grote swarte] gekoop
and Piet has a big-e black-e bought

c. *en Piet het ['n groot swart] gekoop
and Piet has a big black bought

d. *en Piet het ['n groote swart] gekoop
and Piet has a big-e black bought
(Corver & van Koppen 2011: 382)

Apart from the element *-e*, Afrikaans has a second strategy—the use of the pronominal *een* "one."

(117) Jan het ['n wit konyn] gekoop . . .
Jan has a white rabbit bought . . .

a. en Gert het ['n swart konyn] gekoop.
and Gert has a black rabbit bought

b. en Gert het ['n swart **een**] gekoop.
and Gert has a black one bought

c. en Gert het ['n swart*(e)] gekoop.
and Gert has a black-e bought.

d. *en Gert het ['n swarte **een**] gekoop.
and Gert has a black-e one bought

"Jan has bought a white rabbit and Gert bought a black rabbit/a black one."
(Corver & van Koppen 2011: 380)

Conditions on Noun Ellipsis in English 83

Interestingly, *een* and the suffix are in complementary distribution (example 117d), which makes the parallel between *-e* and the pronominal form *een* evident.

Corver and van Koppen's claim that *-e* is just an apparent inflectional ending that has a pronominal status can be applied to the German cases as well. Suppose that gender is the relevant category that needs to be expressed in the German noun phrase. If it is morphologically expressed on an adjective or a determiner, the empty noun remains silent because it is redundant (deletion under adjacency). In those cases where the adjacent element is unspecified for gender, that is, where it is uninflected, the empty noun becomes overt and is spelled out as *-es* (neuter) or *-er* (masculine). Hence, the element that only shows up in elliptical noun phrases can be analyzed along the lines of English *one*—it is a nominal element rather than an inflectional suffix.

4.4 SUMMARY

This chapter identified two conditions on noun ellipsis: a semantico-pragmatic one and a morphosyntactic one. The former was stated in terms of a contrast condition, stating that the antecedent noun phrase and the one containing the anaphoric form have to be nonidentical. Nonidentity can apply either at the lexical or at the referential level. It was argued that these conditions hold for both anaphoric forms, that is, the silent empty noun and the overt empty noun *one*. The analysis of the morphosyntactic conditions follows from the properties of *one*, an overt empty noun that expresses countability. Being devoid of lexical meaning, it is phonologically deleted if an adjacent element is specified for countability. This is due to a haplological principle: Expression of redundant features on adjacent elements leads to deletion of the second element (unless they are lexical, of course). Syntactic haplology does not presuppose phonological identity or similarity.

The deletion process is optional in terms of nonplural quantifiers and adjectives; in the case of elements that are [+plural] it is (predominantly) obligatory (see note 20). In terms of mass noun phrases the same mechanism applies, but the two types of phrases differ in that no overt empty noun for the latter syntactic environment exists.

This analysis is incompatible with a conception of *one* as a classifier. It also rejects the idea that *one* is inserted to license noun ellipsis. Rather, *one* is always present in the structure. It is deleted under certain conditions rather than inserted for certain purposes. Although this does not make an empirical difference, it has theoretical consequences. The relevant question is not under which conditions a silent noun can be licensed but rather which conditions have to be met in order to delete *one*.

These observations were related to nominal classification. A structural view of countability was adopted, which assumes that mass and count noun phrases differ structurally, in that only the latter comprise the functional

84 *The Elliptical Noun Phrase in English*

category number. It was argued that *one* is the phonological realization of a silent noun combining with number morphology. The analysis was extended to noun ellipsis in German, for which gender was argued to be the relevant aspect of noun classification. Apparent inflectional suffixes in elliptical noun phrases were assumed to be phonological realizations of a silent noun encoding gender, in analogy to English *one*.

The model developed here is much simpler than those outlined in Chapter 3. The most obvious advantage is that the elision mechanism follows directly from general structural properties of the nominal domain, and that it interacts with a feature on the licensor. At the same time, this accounts for the distributional restrictions on *one* and the requirement that the licensor must be adjacent to the ellipsis site.

5 Adjectival Modifiers in Elliptical Noun Phrases

In Chapter 2, it was pointed out that it is by no means uncontroversial as to which adjectives[1] allow for a silent noun and that the existence of noun ellipsis with descriptive adjectives is often denied in the literature. On the other hand, Payne and Huddleston (2002), for example, claim that certain semantic types of adjectives, such as those denoting color or provenance, allow for noun ellipsis. It was also pointed out that when it comes to the licensing of silent nouns, reference is made to contextual factors—Bouchard (2002) attributes English noun ellipsis phenomena to salient contexts in which a "sharp contrast" is expressed (Bouchard 2002: 225).

In Chapter 4, it was argued that some adjectives allow for a silent noun more easily than others because they encode countability. Descriptive adjectives, however, hardly qualify as doing so. This gives rise to the following questions. First, is noun ellipsis with descriptive adjectives licit in English at all? And should this actually be the case, is it a particular type of adjective that allows for a silent noun (as claimed by Payne & Huddleston)? Or is it a contrastive context that makes noun ellipsis possible? What do those contexts look like, or, in other words, what makes a contrastive context contrastive?

In order to shed light on these usage-related issues, a search for the silent noun in the *British National Corpus* (BNC) was conducted. The results will be discussed in the course of this chapter. It will be illustrated that the licensing of noun ellipsis with adjectival modifiers is hardly predictable on the basis of a single aspect—rather, a range of different factors contributes to the use of silent nouns.

The structure of this chapter is as follows. The corpus study is laid out in detail in Section 5.1, which presents the difficulties of a search for silent elements and explains why some items (such as demonstrative determines) had to be factored out of the analysis. Section 5.2 shows which adjectival modifiers were found in the corpus. A difference between spoken and written data with respect to noun ellipsis is identified. While spoken language displays a preference for particular adjectives (e.g., color), which relates to salience and physical presence of the referents under consideration, no such generalization can be established for written language. This motivates a closer

86 *The Elliptical Noun Phrase in English*

examination of the contexts in which elliptical noun phrases are used, which is presented in Section 5.3. Three different aspects are addressed: the use of ellipsis in taxonomies (Section 5.3.1.1), lexical relations between modifiers (Section 5.3.1.2), and further lexical and structural means to keep different referents apart (Section 5.3.1.3). It is argued that contextual limitation of sets of referents allows for identification of the sets (and their mass-count properties) more easily (Section 5.3.2). A subsequent analysis of taxonomizing contexts presented in Section 5.4 reveals that silent nouns are preferred in these particular constructions. It is shown that accessibility of antecedents is not the crucial factor here. Two possible explanations are presented: preference for a silent noun with abstract antecedents, and generic reference as being not fully compatible with the classifying properties of number on *one*. Section 5.5 shows that accessibility theory can account for the distribution of nominal heads (lexical, silent, *one*) in contexts where all three forms are equally licit.[2]

5.1 CONDUCTING A CORPUS STUDY ON NOUN ELLIPSIS

This section illustrates how the corpus search was designed. It also outlines the difficulties that a search for silent, that is, nonexistent, elements posits. Some of these problems were circumvented; others led to the exclusion of certain items from the search. The reader who is not interested in these methodological issues should feel free to skip this section.

The unclear data situation in the literature suggests that noun ellipsis with adjectival modifiers is a marginal phenomenon in English and that a useful set of data can be found in a rather large corpus. A further requirement besides size was parts-of-speech (POS) tagging, because the category of adjectives was searched for. Hence, the *British National Corpus* was chosen because it is POS tagged and comprises 100 million words.

The query for elliptical noun phrases was, loosely speaking, set as comprising an article and an adjective followed by anything but a noun. Unfortunately, the CLAWS-5 tag set does not contain tags for silent categories; therefore, the search string became quite complex as illustrated in example (1), where the string is broklen up into its three components, which will be explained in what follows.

(1) _AT0 (_AJ0| _VVN| _VVG) (_AT0| _AVQ| _CJS| _CJT| _DPS| _DTQ|
    _EX0| _ITJ| _PNP| _PNQ| _PNX| _POS| _PRF| _PRP| .| !| \?| ;| _PUR|
    _TO0| _VBB| _VBD| _VBG| _VBI| _VBN| _VDB| _VDD| _VDG| _VBZ|
    _VDI| _VDN| _VDZ| _VHD| _VHB| _VHG| _VHI| _VHN| _VHZ|
    _VM0| _VVB| _VVD| _VVG| _VVI| _VVZ| _XX0)

  a. **Determiner** _AT0
  b. **Adjectival element** (_AJ0| _VVN| _VVG)

Adjectival Modifiers in Elliptical Noun Phrases 87

c. **Nonnominal element** (_AT0| _AVQ| _CJS| _CJT| _DPS| _DTQ| _
EX0| _ITJ| _PNP| _PNQ| _PNX| _POS| _PRF| _PRP| .| !| \?| ;| _PUR|
_TO0| _VBB| _VBD| _VBG| _VBI| _VBN| _VDB| _VDD| _VDG|
_VBZ| _VDI| _VDN| _VDZ| _VHD| _VHB| _VHG| _VHI| _VHN|
_VHZ| _VM0| _VVB| _VVD| _VVG| _VVI| _VVZ| _XX0)

This makeup of the query is the result of several factors. First, AT0 (that is *the, a, an* and *no*) was chosen as the only determiner because the tag comprising demonstratives and the like, DT0, renders a multitude of results where the determiner itself is already followed by a gap, which is then post-modified by an adjective phrase. Compare the following examples:

(2) a. Standards were variable, of course, and first the cinema and then television wiped out a lot of bad theatre as well as **some good.** (BNC, A06 2402)

b. Status of all rooms, including **those ready for use,** can be displayed and adjusted at the Hotel Manager workstation. (BNC, A0C 734)

c. Amongst items produced by the Imperial War Museum are **some suitable for use during reminiscence sessions.** (BNC, A10 726)

In example (2a), a desirable result is represented—the noun phrase in italics is interpreted as *some good theatre,* and thus there is a gap following the modifier *good.* In example (2b), however, the silent noun follows the first element, the demonstrative determiner—*those rooms ready for use*—and does not occur between the modifying adjective *ready* and its complement (**those ready rooms for use*). The same holds for example (2c); the noun follows *some* rather than the adjective *suitable.* Thus, elements that do not license noun ellipsis had to be chosen as determiner in order to avoid results of the type "determiner adjective no noun," with the silent noun being licensed by the first rather than the second element. Moreover, determinative elements such as *all* can also function as modifiers of adjectives. Example (3) illustrates that in such cases there is no noun phrase but an adjective phrase functioning as predicate:

(3) a. Given that this was **all well-known at the outset** what utter fool would believe there could be any money to be made out of such a system. (BNC, A19 691)

b. In a novel where expectations are **not so much unfulfilled as positively spited,** Shatov's future, his hope, suffers simple tragic extinction with his murder. (BNC, A18 1378)

In this case, the aforementioned problem arises, because *all* and *much* are tagged as DT0, the adjectives *well-known* and *unfulfilled* follow, and the third elements also meet the requirement of being not nominal (*at* is

88   The Elliptical Noun Phrase in English

tagged as PRP and *as* is tagged as CJS). But this does not give us the desired results—another reason for limiting the search to constructions containing an article.

The second part of the search string, (_AJ0| _VVN| _VVG), includes not only adjectives in their base form but also past participle forms of lexical verbs (VVN) and *-ing* forms of lexical verbs (VVG), which can also be used to denote properties.

The third part looks quite complex as it contains all the tags that stand for nonnominal elements. However, some other elements such as PUN, which comprises the comma, had to be excluded because this yields too many instances of stacked adjectival modification—see example (4). Adjectives as well as participles were excluded for the same reason, as illustrated in examples (5) and (6).

(4)   She is **a small, passionate, very striking young woman** with deep shining black eyes and a glittering smile, talking ten to the dozen in a strong Moroccan accent. (BNC, A03 811)

(5)   The doctor, universally known as "Hubert," was rotund, but it was a jolly bouncing roundness, not like **the disgusting pot-bellied men** who don't know whether to wear their trousers above or below their pots. (BNC, ABW 1019)

(6)   Her scrunched up face made her look as if she was wearing **a perpetual mirthless grin.** (BNC, ABW 841)

In example (4), the string *a small,* is given as result. Here the comma is not followed by an ellipsis site because the lexical noun occurs after four preceding adjectives. In example (5), the third position in the search string is occupied by another element tagged as AJ0, *pot-bellied;* the lexical noun then appears in the fourth position. The same problem occurs with participles in example (6)—again, a premodifying element fills the third slot and the nominal head follows in position four.

Because of this, the tags VVN, VVG, and AJ0 were excluded from the third position. PUN was excluded as well; in order to capture the cases of noun ellipsis at the end of a syntactic boundary, the full stop, the semicolon, the question mark, and the exclamation mark were accommodated in the third part of the search string.

However, it is thinkable that there are instances of a silent noun being followed by a comma. These cases would remain unnoticed in the above configuration. This issue was solved by another search with the same configuration but with an additional comma between the second and the third part of the search string:

(7)   _AT0 (_AJ0| _VVN| _VVG) \, (_AT0| _AVQ| _CJS| _CJT| _DPS|
      _DTQ| _EX0| _ITJ| _PNP| _PNQ| _PNX| _POS| _PRF| _PRP| .| !| \?| ;|

Adjectival Modifiers in Elliptical Noun Phrases 89

_PUR| _TO0| _VBB| _VBD| _VBG| _VBI| _VBN| _VDB| _VDD| _VDG|
_VBZ| _VDI| _VDN| _VDZ| _VHD| _VHB| _VHG| _VHI| _VHN|
_VHZ| _VM0| _VVB| _VVD| _VVG| _VVI| _VVZ| _XX0)

This search string does not provide undesired results of the type in examples (4) to (6), because now there are four positions in the string and the fourth is neither nominal nor adjectival.

The first search rendered 26,619 hits in 3263 different texts, and the second one returned 4753 hits in 1893 different texts. The total of 31,372 hits were then analyzed manually to exclude instances of the Human Construction and the Abstract Construction in order to find the instances of "proper" elliptical noun phrases, that is, an instance of noun ellipsis with an antecedent either in the same clause, the superordinate or subordinate clause, or the broader context. Further elements that were excluded were some adjectives that do not denote properties such as *other, next,* and *following*.[3] As pointed out throughout this work, these discourse-referential adjectives readily allow for noun ellipsis and can thus be factored out in this search.

Another factor that had to be taken into account was the fact that the BNC was tagged automatically; hence, the modifiers of silent nouns could have been tagged not as adjectives but as nouns, because they are preceded by a determiner and not followed by an overt noun.[4] The CLAWS-5 tag set includes ambiguity tags, and thus a further search was conducted where AJ0 was replaced by AJ0-NN1 and NN1-AJ0. This query yielded another 42,285 hits. Given this large number of matches, which would have to be sorted manually, another strategy had to be chosen. The first one thousand most frequent adjectives in the BNC were taken and inserted in the search string tagged as NN1—as common nouns.[5] This search returned a manageable number of hits.

Another aspect to be considered was plurality. In example (8), the antecedent *pest* bears plural morphology but it is not clear whether the elliptical noun phrase has to be interpreted as singular or plural.

(8) How safe is the new farming method of introducing new pests to fight **the old**? (BNC, EFF 2123)

In order to check whether the modifiers can take plural morphology or not, which would indicate an A-to-N category shift, it would be desirable to have clear cases of plurality. Therefore, in another search the article (AT0) was replaced by a cardinal numeral (CRD). This search returned 2196 hits from which some insightful instances could be extracted.

As pointed out in Chapter 1, a corpus search is a useful tool for examining the linguistic context in which a particular phenomenon occurs. However, the above description of how the search was conducted already indicates that several problems had to be dealt with.

90   *The Elliptical Noun Phrase in English*

The most severe issue certainly is the required manual analysis. There is no other way of recovering the antecedent of the silent noun than to look at the linguistic context. In most cases, the antecedent is provided within the same clause, but, in some instances, syntactic boundaries were crossed, and thus the larger linguistic context had to be analyzed. Moreover, within the spoken data, unidentifiable nonlinguistic antecedents appeared. In some cases, it was indiscernible what the noun phrases refer to. These hits had to be excluded from the analysis as well. Furthermore, instances of the Human Construction and the Abstract Construction had to be sorted out. To sum up, the manual analysis bears two drawbacks. First, it is a time-consuming procedure; second the gathering of the data heavily depends on the researcher's interpretation and intuitions. In addition, some of the above configurations returned a number of hits that was not manageable in a manual analysis. This caused some constructions to be absent from the analysis, and the data to be discussed below do not represent the full picture of noun ellipsis in the BNC.

A minor problem is the absence of tags for empty categories such as silent nouns, which is because a tag for an empty category presupposes a certain theoretical stance on noun ellipsis. However, this problem could be circumvented as described above. A more serious problem was the inconsistency of the tags. The second element in the determiner modifier silent noun construction was tagged as adjective or as common noun. Especially the latter posed a problem, as indicated in the previous section. Recall that the thousand adjectives that ranked highest in terms of overall frequency were picked and searched for with a common noun tag. This implies that almost one hundred thousand other items tagged as positive adjectives in the BNC had to be excluded purely for methodological reasons (see note 4). Needless to say, a search for an element tagged as determiner followed by an element tagged as common noun would have been senseless, as this would also have returned every single noun phrase without a premodifying element in the corpus.

Spoken data also brought about a particular problem for the search—the search string is not affected by utterance boundaries and turn taking. Thus, speaker A might be interrupted by speaker B after having uttered a string of words that qualify as the above phenomenon. However, these hits have to be discarded, as it is not discernable whether the speaker would have used an overt nominal element or not. The extract from file J8B below illustrates the matter: Iris interrupts Robert in the moment he uses a noun phrase (*a different _*). Therefore, it is not clear whether a noun would have been used if the overlap and the resulting interruption had not taken place.

(9) Robert 85   You must've got an extra sheet than me because one of the things I was moaning about this morning <-|-> erm, maybe you've got **a different** <-|->

Iris   86   <-|-> Do you want a copy of this?

Adjectival Modifiers in Elliptical Noun Phrases 91

Similarly, the speaker can make a pause and rephrase the initial conception of the noun phrase:

(10) In other words it's **a new <pause> it's something** which is not done directly from the computer but which is using information the computer provides. (BNC, F7A)

Due to the repetition with the noun phrase's head position being filled in the second clause, it is more likely that the speaker would not have used an elliptical phrase. Rather, he hesitates because he does not know how to name the referent and hence chooses the indefinite pronoun *something* instead.

However, despite the issues outlined above, the analysis yielded a useful set of data to be discussed in what follows.

5.2 ADJECTIVES USED IN ELLIPTICAL NOUN PHRASES

The BNC search yielded 965 results matching the above requirements. Hence, noun ellipsis is indeed licit with adjectival modifiers in English. Spoken language files yielded 186 hits, and the other 779 came from written texts. In Table 5.1, the different adjectives are ordered according to the number of their occurrences in elliptical noun phrases. Due to space restrictions, those that occur twice and only once, respectively, are not listed as separate entries.

The table displays a multitude of different modifiers—335 altogether. In Chapter 2 it was pointed out that, according to Payne and Huddleston (2002), particular semantic classes of adjectives can license a silent noun (see Section 2.1.3). Those are adjectives denoting basic physical properties, such as color or nationality. The table reveals that it is in fact color adjectives that occur frequently as modifiers in elliptical noun phrases: *Red* appears 68 times, *blue* 47 times, *black* occurs 29 times, there are 21 hits for *yellow*, 19 for *white*, 11 for *green* and 11 for *grey*. Furthermore, there are 7 instances of *pink* and 4 of *brown*, and among the adjectives that are not listed separately, there are eight further color adjectives (*lemon* appears twice and there is one hit for *silver-grey, black pied, red pied, gold* and *golden*, and *white and red*, respectively). Thus, 225 instances of the 965 hits are color adjectives, and, hence, the result apparently mirrors the claim put forward by Payne and Huddleston. This is seemingly corroborated by the fact that *old* and *new*, "modifiers denoting basic physical properties such as age" (ibid.: 417) are also quite frequent. However, this conclusion is too premature, as the following discussion shows.

In order to spot potential flaws, a look at differences in distribution within spoken and written texts proves insightful. Table 5.2 summarizes the findings for spoken language. Table 5.3 displays the frequency of adjectives modifying silent nouns in written texts.

Color adjectives constitute 129 of the 186 hits[6] in spoken texts and 96 of the 779 hits[7] that stem from written texts. Thus, adjectives denoting

92 *The Elliptical Noun Phrase in English*

Table 5.1 Adjectival modifiers of silent nouns in the BNC

Modifier	Number of hits	Modifier	Number of hits	Modifier	Number of hits
old	108	*positive*	7	*basic*	3
red	68	*southern*	7	*British*	3
new	68	*general*	6	*eastern*	3
blue	47	*large*	6	*English*	3
black	29	*private*	6	*horizontal*	3
yellow	21	*dominant*	5	*inner*	3
upper	20	*normal*	5	*internal*	3
white	19	*psychological*	5	*international*	3
good	18	*social*	5	*particular*	3
bad	17	*brown*	4	*rational*	3
small	13	*economic*	4	*Scottish*	3
green	11	*European*	4	*specific*	3
grey	11	*local*	4	*technical*	3
left	9	*negative*	4	*theoretical*	3
outer	9	*sexual*	4	*verbal*	3
political	8	*spoken*	4	*young*	3
long	7	*vertical*	4		
northen	7	*written*	4	40 modifiers	2
physical	7	*active*	3	238 modifiers	1
pink	7	*backward*	3		
Total		335 modifiers		965 hits	

Table 5.2 Adjectival modifiers of silent nouns in spoken language

Modifier	Number of hits	Modifier	Number of hits	Modifier	Number of hits
red	54	*pink*	4	*local*	2
blue	34	*long*	3	*outer*	2
black	12	*old*	3	*thick*	2
yellow	10	*big*	2	*upper*	2
white	6	*different*	2		
green	5	*grey*	2	35 modifiers	1
new	4	*inner*	2		
Total		53 modifiers		186 hits	

Adjectival Modifiers in Elliptical Noun Phrases 93

Table 5.3 Adjectival modifiers of silent nouns in written language

Modifier	Number of hits	Modifier	Number of hits	Modifier	Number of hits
old	105	*northern*	7	*long*	4
new	64	*outer*	7	*negative*	4
upper	18	*physical*	7	*normal*	4
black	17	*positive*	7	*sexual*	4
good	17	general	6	*spoken*	4
bad	16	*green*	6	*theoretical*	4
red	14	*large*	6	*vertical*	4
blue	13	*southern*	6	*written*	4
small	13	*dominant*	5		
white	13	*private*	5		
yellow	11	*psychological*	5	14 modifiers	3
grey	9	*social*	5	38 modifiers	2
left	8	*economic*	4	223 modifiers	1
political	8	*European*	4		
Total		311 modifiers		779 hits	

color make up 69.35 percent of the hits within spoken texts and only 12.32 percent of those in written texts.

Hence, the notion of a basic property denoted by the adjective is more relevant for spoken language than for written. This is not surprising, because these properties allow for a distinction among different referents more easily than other properties, such as for example value. Colors are hardly gradable—an object is either red or it is not red—and they denote a property that is not subject to interpretation, in contrast to adjectives of value. If a speaker tells the addressee that he or she needs a red (one), the addressee is more likely to identify the objects to which the description applies than if he or she was informed that the speaker needs an interesting (one).

The difference in distribution between spoken and written language derives from distinct discourse situations. The color adjectives found in spoken language stem from settings where the referents are physically present in the text-external world. For example, 39 instances of the color adjectives originate from file FYA 1233 onward—a transcript of a teacher-student conversation on probability calculation that centers on red and blue beads that are drawn from a bag. The frequent use of *blue* and *red* in the conversation is illustrated in example (11):

(11) John   1371   Right.

               1372   So the chance of getting **a red,** is one in four.

94   *The Elliptical Noun Phrase in English*

Chris	1373	Ah.
John	1374	The chance of getting **a blue?**
Chris	1375	Is three in four.
John	1376	And the chance of getting either **a red** or **a blue,** If I say, Here you are, I'm gonna you've got this bag and it's got **three blue** and **one red** in it.
	1377	And I'm gonna pick one at random, and I'm gonna have this bet with you that I will get either **a red** or **a blue.** (BNC, FYA)

The discourse topic is a number of beads in different colors that are put into a bag as well as the likelihood to draw beads of a certain color, which also explains the frequent use of a numeral with a color adjective:

(12) Bag A has got **three blue,** and **one red.** (BNC, FYA 1346)

(13) Bag B's got **three blue** and **three red.** (BNC, FYA 1573)

(14) We put it in the second bag, and that's now **three red.** (BNC, FYA 1444)

(15) Looking at this one, if we pulled a red one out of bag A and put it into bag B, bag B would now have **three blue,** and **four red.** (BNC, FYA 1424)

Similarly, 26 hits derive from one file part (BNC, KBK 5000 and onward), where the discourse centers on a game involving balls of different colors (probably snooker). A further discourse context involves playing a game, referred to as the "caterpillar game" by the speakers (BNC, KBW 5279). Every player chooses a color: *I'm gonna be yellow this time* (BNC, KBW 5286). The task seems to be collecting different colored objects that are not specified linguistically (*Oh I've got lots of yellow things* (BNC, KBW 5479)).[8]

(16) I think I'll be **a green.** (BNC, KBW 5563)

(17) just cos I saved you **a green** there love. (BNC, KBW 5569)

(18) I need **a red!** (BNC, KBW 5498)

Thus, in spoken language noun ellipsis is used when the referent is very salient due to its presence in the text-external world and due to its topicality. The related concept of accessibility will be discussed in subsection 5.4.2 and Section 5.5, but suffice it to say at this point that in these contexts, noun ellipsis serves the purpose of linguistic economy: Speakers try to avoid redundant information.[9]

In terms of the adjectives used in elliptical noun phrases in written language, such generalizations can hardly be established. Adjectives denoting age, another basic property, feature prominently in the written texts (105 hits for *old* and 64 hits for *new*), but this is only an apparent parallel to the cases in spoken language. A look at the frequency lists of nongraded adjectives (AJ0) for written texts in the BNC reveals that this ranking reflects their overall appearance in the corpus: *Other* is the most frequent adjective (116,786, and recall that this one was excluded from the analysis), followed by *new* (107,224), *good* (60,421), and *old* (46,857). A chi-square test indicates that there is a correlation between the frequency of occurrence in elliptical noun phrases and overall frequency in the corpus for *old* and *new* (χ^2 = 81,604, df = 1, p < 0,001). Therefore, the analysis does not show a particular distribution of semantic adjective classes in terms of written language, which makes a closer examination of contextual aspects indispensable.

5.3 CONTEXTUAL LIMITATIONS OF SETS: TAXONOMIES AND LEXICAL RELATIONS

In this section, the contexts in which the elliptical noun phrase occurs are given consideration. The first part is descriptive—it shows two uses of elliptical noun phrases that featured prominently among the results. The first will be referred to as the Taxonomizing Construction (example 19). It has been mentioned several times as a context that makes noun ellipsis licit both in English and French. The example was first presented by Sleeman (1996) and quoted by Bouchard (2002: 231) and Alexiadou and Gengel (forthcoming).

(19) Parmi les tableaux exposés dans ce musée, je distinguerai trois catégories: **les magnifiques, les bizarres** et **les affreux.**
Among the paintings exhibited in this museum I will distinguish three categories: the magnificent [ones], the strange[ones], and the awful [ones].
(Sleeman 1996: 16n3)

The second context to be discussed pertains to the use of binary pairs of adjectives as modifiers of the antecedent and the silent noun. In addition, other contrast-encoding devices will be presented. The remainder of this chapter shows how the findings can be brought in line with the claims made in Chapter 4.

5.3.1 Different Uses of Elliptical Noun Phrases

5.3.1.1 Taxonomizing Contexts

The corpus study revealed that the construction in example (19) is a rather productive one in English: 136 out of the 965 modifiers occurred in this

96 *The Elliptical Noun Phrase in English*

particular setting. In this construction, a class is denoted by the antecedent, then different members of this class are specified.

The antecedent is usually accompanied by a numeral that indicates the cardinality of the set, as in examples (20) to (24):

(20) A narrow path led between <u>the two waters</u>, **the wild** and **the domesticated.** (BNC, ADM 409)

(21) and as Hobsbawm (1964, p. 32) remarked there now seem to be <u>three or four alternative routes out of the primitive communal system</u>: **the oriental, the ancient, the Germanic** (or more broadly, feudal), and less clearly articulated, **the Slavonic.** (BNC, H9F 292)

(22) Habermas reveals <u>three such interests</u>. **The technical,** which corresponds to the activity of the nomological sciences, **the practical,** which corresponds to the hermeneutic sciences, and **the emancipatory,** which corresponds to the critical sciences. (BNC, CGY 1035)

(23) <u>These threatening contacts</u> are of <u>two</u> kinds: **the difficult** and **the sympathetic.** (CKS 1066)

(24) There are <u>two versions of the anthropic principle</u>, **the weak** and **the strong.** (BNC, H78 1120)

There are other ways to indicate the number of referents the set consists of, such as the modifier *dual* in example (25) and determinative *both* in example (26).

(25) This, she points out, provides useful clarification of the analysis of <u>the dual functions of language</u>, **the cognitive** and **the performative,** central to Paul de Man's work. (BNC, ATA 1308)

(26) <u>Both aspects of language development</u>, **the personal** and **the social,** contribute to giving pupils power over their own lives. (BNC, CCV 334)

The size of the set can also be determined in a vaguer sense by the use of an indefinite quantifier.

(27) <u>Various types of criminal</u>—**the political, the habitual** and **the recidivist, the feeble-minded, the inebriate, the juvenile**—were all differentiated as separate specimens in the taxonomies of the new science of criminology. (BNC, AS6 602)

(28) Leadership is also apparent in <u>many different spheres of activity</u>—**the military, the political, the organisational** and so on—and it may exist at different levels. (BNC, GVN 1107)

Adjectival Modifiers in Elliptical Noun Phrases   97

In some instances of the construction, however, no such indication is given, as the following examples display:

(29) What do you consider to be <u>the most formative experiences of your life</u> so far, **the painful** as well as **the good?** (BNC, GE 285)

(30) Note down <u>the points that strike you about this delivery system</u>, **the good** as **the bad.** (BNC, CAP 1545)

Note that this Taxonomizing Construction always has a rather fixed form and meaning: An antecedent, which supplies the ellipsis site with an interpretation, is introduced. This noun establishes a class of potential referents. In most cases, this set is narrowed down in size by a numeral or a similar element. Then at least two subsets of that set are identified with elliptical noun phrases coordinated by *and*. Those conjuncts mostly take the definite article and contain an adjectival modifier.[10] The two subsets made reference to by the phrases containing the ellipsis site are interpreted as available subkinds, hence the label Taxonomizing Construction. Thus, this construction has a rather fixed grammatical form and a very particular meaning, namely a categorizing function.[11]

The context of this construction strongly suggests that the noun phrases under consideration are indeed elliptical. In example (31), both elliptical phrases of the conjunct, *the consultative* and *the democratic,* are taken up again in the discourse, but the head position is filled by the lexical noun *approach,* which serves as antecedent for the ellipsis sites.

(31) One can identify <u>two broad types of approach</u>, which I will call **the democratic** and **the consultative.** In a democratic **approach,** all sources of knowledge are given similar roles in the control structure. When an anaphor is being resolved, each source can, at least in principle, propose new candidate referents, contribute positively or negatively to the score of each candidate referent, and in some cases rule candidates out altogether. In a **consultative approach,** one knowledge source, typically encoding some kind of focusing information, is given a special role. (BNC, B2X 697–700)

This may be taken as indication that the use of the elliptical noun phrases is restricted to this particular construction. However, the following example demonstrates that this is not borne out. All three referential expressions of the conjunct are repeated: Two have their head realized as a lexical noun, but one of them still contains an silent noun.

(32) Comte argued that human thought passes through <u>three stages</u>: **the theological, the metaphysical,** and **the positive. The theological stage** he associated with militarism, **the metaphysical** with juristic thought, and **the positive stage** with industrialism. (BNC, EAJ 666,7)

98 *The Elliptical Noun Phrase in English*

The BNC study revealed a further mechanism that is very similar to the aforementioned one. An antecedent comes with a numeral, which delimits the set; then different referents that make up the set are listed. This is illustrated in examples (33) to (36).

(33) . . . while in the six-part sinfonia which follows these instruments are joined by <u>6 lutes</u> (**three large** and **three small**) (BNC, GUH 627)

(34) The Gracious Speech contains <u>three Bills on education</u>; **two English** and **one Scottish.** (BNC, HHW 2310)

(35) the PUSC won an absolute majority, winning 29 of the 57 seats against 25 for the PLN and <u>three for smaller parties</u> (**one left-wing, two regional**) (BNC, HKR 519)

(36) and then only the buzz of the chain free-wheeling and the rush of the air: and <u>two stars</u>, **a red, a white,** shooting down the dark tunnel of road between the hedges (BNC, H9G 1681)

Although they look similar, the Taxonomizing Construction and these enumerations are not identical: There is no definite article but an element that indicates cardinality (numerals as in examples 33–35 and the indefinite article in example 36). Still, these two phenomena display the same mechanism: A set is defined explicitly before a referent is identified. Therefore, the enumeration mechanism will be considered a subtype of the Taxonomizing Construction.

5.3.1.2 Lexical Relations

The second aspect to be discussed concerns the lexical relation between the adjective modifying the antecedent noun (or anywhere else within the immediate context, see below), and the one modifying the silent noun. Two types of relations were distinguished. First, it was analyzed whether the adjectives stem from the same semantic class (semantic class as used here refers to categorization according to denotation, e.g., color; see Dixon 1982). In a second step, these modifiers were further divided into clearly antonymic and nonantonymic cases. Antonymic as used here is understood in a rather strict sense of the term; it refers to either binary pairs of nongradable antonyms or to the opposite endpoints on a scale of gradable notions.

Interestingly, 685 modifiers are of the first type, that is, the antecedent and the silent noun, are modified by the adjectives of the same type, as illustrated by the following examples:

(37) and delays rapidly reached six months on <u>the French side</u> and three months on **the British.** (BNC, BMJ 249)

Adjectival Modifiers in Elliptical Noun Phrases 99

(38) the Latvian rouble had the same value as **the Russian** (BNC, K1B 2743)

(39) The flight of the red squirrels from **the grey.** (BNC, EFF 1838)

(40) But it was left to Oxford Hawks in the gold shirts and Gloucester City in **the red** to battle it out for the minor places in a Central South (BNC, K1B 2743)

In examples (37) and (38), there are two modifiers denoting nationality that are used with the antecedent and the elliptical noun phrase: There is a French side and a British side (37), as well as two types of ruble, a Russian and a Latvian (37). This shows that the modifier used with the antecedent introduces the property according to which the set (denoted by the antecedent) is categorized. The other two examples display the same for color adjectives; of the class of squirrels the red and the grey ones are picked out, and in example (40), there are gold shirts and red shirts selected of the class of shirts.

The total of adjectives of the same type, 685, comprises those 430 that are in antonymic relationship to one in the immediate context. Among them are adjectives that denote what Sleeman refers to as basic notions: *Good* and *bad*, *old* and *new*, and *small* and *large* occur as binary pairs. An example for each of the above as modifier of a silent noun is provided:

(41) a. One day, they met in the second class compartment of a train—; unemployed but taking the *bad* days as cheerfully as **the** *good* (BNC, EVF 206)

  b. They are trying to isolate their *good* properties from **the** *bad.* (BNC, AKL 309)

(42) a. Because the innovator has for enemies all those who have done well under the *old* conditions . . . and lukewarm defenders in those who may do well under **the** *new.* (BNC, CKS 169)

  b. It is clear that local government promises to be an even worse headache for the *new* government than it was for **the** *old.* (BNC, AK2 284)

(43) a. Thus, the right of the *large* nation could deny that of **the** *small.* (BNC, ANT 680)

  b. it should take into account the public as well as the private sector, the *small* practitioner as well as **the** *large.* (BNC, APX 169)

In addition to the basic adjectives, modifiers that indicate the position of a referent relative to another, such as *vertical-horizontal, left-right,*

100   *The Elliptical Noun Phrase in English*

inner-outer, northern-southern, upper-low/lower, are used in elliptical noun phrases:

(44) In Figure 1.1 we have represented the holism-individualism range on the *vertical* axis and the explaining-understanding contrast on **the** *horizontal* (BNC, EDD 68)

(45) Practise this the full length of the training hall and then switch feet, keeping the *right* foot in place and stepping out with **the** *left* (BNC, GVF 508)

(46) The library consisted of two rooms, but the only entry to the *inner room* was through **the** *outer.* (BNC, B0U 2432)

(47) Serpens is divided into two parts, Caput (the Head) in the *northern* hemisphere and Cauda (the Body) in **the** *southern.* (BNC, EAW 595)

(48) Another factor is that the characteristics of intervals are greatly increased in the *low* registers and decreased in **the** *upper* (BNC, GVJ 1486)

Interestingly, there are also pairs of modifiers that clearly do not fall into the class of basic terms, among them *spoken-written* and *private-public,* and rather complex ones such as *brain-damaged* as opposed to *normal,* and *developing* and *developed,* to name but a few.

(49) Some individuals spend more time with the *written* language than they do with **the** *spoken.* (BNC, F9V 227)

(50) All such sources of conflict are familiar to those in the *public* sector as much as they are to those in **the** *private.* (BNC, HTF 1312)

(51) A positive symptom is something that happens in the *brain-damaged animal* that doesn't happen in **the** *normal* (BNC, CMH 926)

(52) In the last two decades world production of electricity has roughly doubled, with the *developing* nations pulling towards overtaking **the** *developed.* (BNC, AB6 563)

This antonymic relation is not necessarily restricted to antecedent modifier and modifier of the silent noun but can also hold between modifiers in several elliptical noun phrases, as example (53) shows:

(53) But not all mosquitoes that breed in puddles or water pots are vectors of malaria, and it takes a competent entomologist to distinguish **the** *dangerous* from **the** *harmless* and to carry out this "species sanitation." (BNC, B7E 413)

Adjectival Modifiers in Elliptical Noun Phrases 101

It should be pointed out that the instances of lexical relations discussed in the previous section and the syntactic configurations analyzed in this section are not mutually exclusive. Examples such as (24), replicated here as (54), show that within the Taxonomizing Construction antonymic relations may hold between the modifiers.

(54) There are <u>two versions of the anthropic principle,</u> **the *weak*** and **the *strong*.** (BNC, H78 1120) (= example 24)

This signals that the different aspects outlined here overlap and explains why the number of instances found in the search provided for each case adds up to more than the total of 965 modifiers.

5.3.1.3 Further Means to Express Contrast

So far, two main aspects related to contrast and noun ellipsis have been outlined—lexical relations of the modifiers and different ways to denote classes with subsequent identification of their members. Before these findings are discussed and integrated into the account developed in Chapter 4, a brief look will be taken at further means to induce contrast that feature prominently in the BNC data. Even though these are minor effects and do not contribute significantly to the point to be made, they will be summarized to provide a comprehensive answer to the question of what contrastive contexts might look like.

The aspects to be presented fall into two main categories: syntactic patterns and lexical means. In terms of the latter, use is made of elements that have a contrastive meaning such as predicates expressing similarity or difference like *different (from)*, *compared (to)*, and *compared (with)*.

(55) . . . if <u>the new use</u> is "substantially" *different from* **the old** (BNC, B2D 684)

(56) but secrecy is still a significant feature of <u>the British executive,</u> especially *compared to* **the American.** (BNC, GV5 662)

(57) Certainly the absence of commercially significant rain-forest fruits in <u>the New World,</u> *compared with* **the Old,** . . . (BNC, J18 413)

In the above example, an adjective expresses a relation between two referents. A similar case can also be found within the verbal domain—there are a range of verb-preposition/particle combinations that distinguish referents from each other, as becomes evident in the following examples:

(58) Pascoe could *tell* <u>a good lie</u> *from* **a bad.** (BNC, FP7 2011)

(59) . . . the element of indecency is used to *separate* <u>the sexual offence</u> *from* **the non-sexual.** (BNC, ACJ 1119)

102　*The Elliptical Noun Phrase in English*

(60) . . . to provide ammunition for an attack on schools <u>whose approach to learning</u> *diverged from* the traditional (BNC, CLY 264)

(61) On an international scale Louth sits right on the line *dividing* <u>the Eastern hemisphere</u> *from* the Western. (BNC, ECR 446)

(62) Thompson's purpose here is *to contrast* <u>the eighteenth century's passive materialism</u>, reflected in Owen's views, with the active, . . . (BNC, EF4 506)

Verbal constructions such as *tell from, separate from,* and *contrast with,* to name a few, make a contrastive relation between referents explicit.

The other structural way to enhance contrast is the use of parallelism. Consider the following examples:

(63) the more recent folk-songs of America, which were borne out of economic collapse (on <u>the white hand</u>), and subservience and racialism (on the black) (BNC, A0P 1347)

(64) <u>The creative and necessary activities</u> are encouraged (even demanded) whilst the destructive are curtailed. (BNC, FE6 164)

In these examples, the noun phrase containing the antecedent and the elliptical noun phrase have similar syntactic roles: In example (63), both phrases are coordinates in complement position to a preposition, and in example (64), each of the two is in subject position of a passive clause. Further contrast is brought about by antonymic adjectives modifying the antecedent and the silent noun. What is more, the participles *encouraged* and *curtailed* denote opposite results of activities. In the following examples, a similar way of enhancing contrast is apparent:

(65) The idea that <u>the northern suite</u> was used in summer and the eastern in winter does not convince. (BNC, CM9 229)

(66) For it was possible, on a reading of Marius' contio in Sallust, to associate <u>the old nobility</u> with inertia, the new with virtue. (BNC, EA7 315)

(67) The first are aimed at <u>the commercial market</u>; the latter at the technical. (BNC, CSV 446)

(68) It has a horizontal division across its pupil which effectively gives it four eyes—<u>the two lower halves</u> for seeing underwater, the two upper for doing so in air (BNC, EFR 1720)

Adjectival Modifiers in Elliptical Noun Phrases 103

In these examples, elliptical noun phrase and antecedent noun phrase have comparable syntactic roles again. In addition, other constituents further incorporate contrast on the lexical level. In example (65), *summer* and *winter* are contrasted, and in example (66), *inertia* and *virtue*, as complements to the same preposition, underline the differences between the two referents contrasted in the proposition. Ellipsis in these examples does not just affect the nominal domain. In examples (66) and (67), instances of gapping appear; the verb (including auxiliaries and infinitival *to*) are elided. In example (68), another case of pronominalization shows up; the pro- form *do so* is substituted for the verb.

5.3.2 Contextual Limitations of Reference Sets

5.3.2.1 The Notion of Classifying Adjectives

In terms of noun ellipsis with descriptive adjectives, reference has been made to the notion of classifying adjectives. I will briefly summarize the main aspects in order to show in how far this concept is applicable to the phenomena described above.

According to Sleeman (1996), classifying adjectives allow for noun ellipsis in French because they are partitive (see also Alexiadou & Gengel [forthcoming] for a similar claim). They are among the so-called N-partitives, that is, they are noninherently partitive elements (see Section 3.3). Sleeman points out that the adjectives most relevant for French noun ellipsis denote basic notions and constitute binary pairs (*big-small, good-bad,* and so forth). Classifying adjectives are defined as "attributive adjectives . . . that express cognitively relevant notions, which give them discriminating properties" (1996: 145). "Cognitively relevant" as used here relates to the basic semantic adjective classes listed by Dixon (1977). Sleeman considers these adjectives to be contrastive and to have a partitive meaning at a cognitive level because their discriminating properties allow for the creation of subsets.

Although Sleeman's proposal remains rather vague on this particular point, a quote from Jones (1993) allows insights into how this might work. According to Jones, these adjectives, which also allow for noun ellipsis in Sardinian, "imply a binary paradigmatic contrast" (1993: 73). In other words, whenever one of these is used, a property of a further referent is implied and becomes contextually active as a set of alternatives to be excluded. The partitive meaning of these adjectives is construed in a similar way to that of discourse-referential adjectives.[12] Their use establishes a relation to another referent, which allows for the silent noun's contents to be recovered via the link to a superset.

As became evident in Section 5.2, a whole range of different modifiers was found in elliptical noun phrases. They range from those discussed above, that is, from absolute adjectives denoting inherent properties of the referent to relative adjectives that express more speaker-oriented properties such as *good* and *bad*. Furthermore, they do not denote basic properties

104 *The Elliptical Noun Phrase in English*

only, as Table 5.1 displays; adjectives such as *psychological, social, active, economic, spoken,* and *written* can hardly be considered to be "cognitively basic notions." However, an analysis of the lexical relations between the adjectives still proves fruitful to explain why the classifying character of an adjective might be considered as licensor of a silent noun.

The first aspect to be looked into is that adjectives of the same type feature prominently as modifiers of silent nouns (685 instances out of 965). This effect is most likely to be pragmatically induced: When two (or more) referents are used within a proposition, some kind of relation is established between them. In Section 4.1, it was pointed out that the modifiers have to express non-identity of the referents, that is, comparison and contrast apply at the domain of the modifier of silent nouns. Hence, the modifiers must denote comparable properties and this is why they qualify as classifying adjectives, which, according to Halliday, "indicates a particular subclass of the thing in question" (1985: 164).

Take the following case of a nonelliptical noun phrase as an illustration:

(69) The red line represents freon eleven and **the green line** freon twelve.
      (BNC, F8G 107)

In example (69), two instances of the class of lines are contrasted—there is a red line and a green line. The distinguishing property of the two objects of the same kind is their color. If a modifier from a different semantic class such as size is used, as (madeup) example (70) shows, the modifiers are still interpreted as being in a contrastive relation.

(70) #The red line represents freon eleven and *the thin line* freon twelve.

Unless red lines can be taken to be thick, or at least as not thin, this utterance is infelicitous. This shows that the requirement of the modifiers being within the same category is not exclusive to noun ellipsis but derives from the contrast condition on anaphoric nominal forms.[13]

What can be construed to be within one category, of course, is speaker- and context-dependent. This is clearly illustrated by the use of the Taxonomizing Construction:

(71) Comte argued that human thought passes through three stages: **the theological, the metaphysical,** and **the positive. The theological stage** he associated with militarism, **the metaphysical** with juristic thought, and **the positive stage** with industrialism. (BNC, EAJ 666,7) (= example 32)

Even if the modifiers are strictly speaking not within one semantic category (such as color, age, or value), they still denote comparable properties, because any kind of property can be used to distinguish a referent from other referents in an appropriate context. Therefore, the above statement

Adjectival Modifiers in Elliptical Noun Phrases 105

has to be revised; the modifiers have to stem from one pragmatic category. This signals what Sleeman remarks in a footnote—"in fact most adjectives classify" (1996: 15n1). However, even though what counts as classifying is speaker-dependent to a large extent, some properties might be recognizable more easily. Color, provenance, and the like are absolute in contrast to the more subjective modifiers, such as adjectives of value (see also Section 5.2 on noun ellipsis in spoken English). Still, some of the latter (such as *bruttu* "dirty, ugly" and *bellu* "beautiful") are included in Jones' (1993: 73f) list of basic adjectives that function as noun ellipsis licensors in Sardinian. This shows that what is understood as basic property or as a liable defining aspect is also flexible cross-linguistically.[14]

To sum up, even though adjectives that denote basic properties allow for an identification of referents more easily, these basic properties leave a large amount of data from the written component unaccounted for. The notion of classifying adjectives is best understood as a pragmatic phenomenon—any adjective can be classifying if the context is right. This suggests that contextual aspects play a more prominent role.[15]

5.3.2.2 Closed Sets of Referents

The Taxonomizing Construction, though not referred to as such, has been presented as an example for noun ellipsis with adjectives in the literature. According to Sleeman, the opposition with further adjectives gives these a classifying character, and Bouchard (2002) argues that the delimitation of the superset establishes a partitive relation that makes a referent identifiable. Bouchard analyzes the construction (example 19) as follows. There are three levels. The first one denotes the set of all possible referents. The second level represents the denotation resulting from the intersection of the adjective and the extension of the noun. On the final level, the determiner picks out a referent of that subset. Next, in terms of the above construction, an additional level is inserted in order to contextually limit the above set of all possible referents. This process is schematized for *the magnificent paintings*:

(72) Level 1: set of all possible referents   {a, b, c, d . . . x, y, z}

       Level 1: set of paintings in museum   {a, b, f, . . . m, r . . . w}

       Level 2: set of MAGNIFICENT   {b, f, . . . m, r}

       Level 3: set from atomization by
            def. plur. Det.   {f, m}

Even though the delimitation of the set of referents certainly plays a role here, the corpus data suggest that it is the numeral that limits the set of referents—*je distinguerai **trois** categories* ("I will distinguish three categories") rather than the restriction to "some magnificent paintings in a particular museum" (Bouchard 2002: 231). This is because in the majority of cases

106 *The Elliptical Noun Phrase in English*

identified above, the cardinality of the superset denoted by the antecedent is explicitly mentioned. Hence, the number of the referents that constitute the set is made explicit. After the set has been established, the different set members are listed. In most instances of the Taxonomizing Construction (in those cases where the exact number of referents is provided), the referents the superset comprises are exhaustively identified:

(73) Habermas reveals <u>three such interests</u>. **The technical,** which corresponds to the activity of the nomological sciences, **the practical,** which corresponds to the hermeneutic sciences, and **the emancipatory,** which corresponds to the critical sciences. (BNC, CGY 1035) (= example 22)

(74) . . . while in the six-part sinfonia which follows these instruments are joined by <u>6</u> <u>lutes</u> (**three large** and **three small**) (BNC, GUH 627) (= example 33)

(75) . . . and then only the buzz of the chain free-wheeling and the rush of the air: and <u>two stars,</u> **a red, a white,** shooting down the dark tunnel of road between the hedges (BNC, H9G 1681) (= example 36)

As example (75) shows, this also holds for the use of the indefinite article in the construction. This contextual limitation of the set of referents and the exhaustive identification of each set member make the individual referents clearly identifiable. Arguably, the mechanism works in a similar way for the use of binary adjective pairs; because they denote opposites they imply duality of a set whose members are listed at the same time.

Furthermore, the use of *one* to disambiguate number and indicate countability is not required. In the Taxonomizing Construction, the numeral (or a similar element) defining the cardinality of the set denoted by the antecedent corresponds to the number of elliptical noun phrases used. In example (73), the set of interests contains three different types, which are each denoted by an elliptical noun phrase. Therefore, the noun phrases in this context can be interpreted as singular without the expression of *one*. In the same vein, the use of binary adjective pairs that imply set-duality with two referential expressions (one elliptical and one containing the antecedent) indicates singularity of the latter. This number disambiguation may further increase the indentifiability of the referents in questions.

5.4 PREFERENCE FOR ELLIPTICAL NOUN PHRASES IN TAXONOMIES

The following subsection examines further aspects of taxonomizing contexts in order to show which factors also contribute to the relaxation of the requirement to use *one*.

Adjectival Modifiers in Elliptical Noun Phrases   107

5.4.1 Realizations of the Head Noun: Lexical, Silent, and *One*

In English, there are three ways to realize an anaphoric head noun: repetition of the lexical head noun, empty noun *one*, and silent empty noun. In the Taxonomizing Construction, the form definite article + adjective + silent noun is preferred. This becomes evident in a search for the construction with consideration of different possible realizations of the nominal head. The basic search string is noun phrase *and* noun phrase. Please note that this does not mean that only two conjuncts are allowed for, because it does not preclude further conjuncts that precede those covered by the search.

The different configurations searched for were as follows: First, the repetition of the lexical noun was included (example 76). In order to keep the number of hits as low as possible (a manual analysis was required again), only singular nouns were allowed for. This does not pose any methodological problems because, as pointed out above, the number of conjuncts matches the total of referents and, hence, each noun phrase is necessarily singular. The second search covered cases where the nominal head is realized as *one* in all conjuncts (example 77). The third was set to find the cases where the head is silent in all conjuncts (example 78). The fourth one aimed at instances of the Taxonomizing Construction with a lexical nominal head in the first conjunct and *one* as head in the second conjunct (example 79). Finally, a search was modeled to detect those instances where the head in the last conjunct is realized as *one* and as a silent empty noun in the preceding one (example 80).

Each search string and its results are outlined below. It should be pointed out that only true instances of the Taxonomizing Construction were taken into account (they were filtered out manually).

(76) Repetition of the lexical noun (= A)

Definites

Search string: the _AJ0 _NN1 and the _AJ0 _NN1

Hits: 8

Examples:

a. As far as I was concerned there were <u>two types of women</u>, **the true type** and **the failed type.** (BNC, CEE 946)

b. <u>Three main classes</u>—**the upper class, the middle class,** and **the working class** will be considered in turn, though as will become clear, the location of the boundaries between these classes is disputed. (BNC, FB6 1454)

c. <u>Two approaches</u> are currently being investigated. These are **the biological approach** and **the biochemical approach.** (BNC, HSD 2025)

108   *The Elliptical Noun Phrase in English*

d. It is already known that the normal reader has at his or her disposal <u>two very different procedures</u> (two very different sets of mental operations) for accomplishing the conversion of print to speech. These are now known as **the lexical procedure** and **the nonlexical procedure.** (BNC, HHY 7382)

e. There are <u>two ways to make profit,</u> **the barbaric way** and **the diplomatic way.** (BNC, EW5 1207)

f. Ingwersen has characterized <u>three types of searches</u>: **the open search, the fixed search,** and **the semi-fixed search.** (BNC, H0S 257)

g. . . . so instead of having <u>two classes,</u> **the working class** and **the upper class** who spent their lives in leisure, in idleness, . . . (BNC, KRJ 9)

h. These activities are considered in the context of the <u>two models of policy making</u>—**the rational model** and **the incremental model**— which were examined in the previous chapter. (BNC, GVN 2007)

Indefinites

<u>Search string</u>: (a|an) _AJ0 _NN1 and (a|an) _AJ0 _NN1

<u>Hits</u>: 4

Examples:

i. . . . implies <u>two criteria of relevance for the selection of stylistic features</u>: **a literary criterion** and **a linguistic criterion.** (BNC, EWA 728)

j. There are <u>two types of indexes</u> to be found in classification schemes: **a relative index** and **a specific index.** (BNC, H99 759)

k. We feel drawn to distinguish <u>two ways of knowing things,</u> **an inward way** and **an outward way.** (BNC, CK1 1288)

l. A small wooden peg called <u>a spile</u> is knocked into the soft core of the shive. <u>Two types</u> are used: **a soft spile** and **a hard spile.** (BNC, A0A 122,3)

(77) Coordination of two phrases containing *one* (= B)

Definites

<u>Search string</u>: the _AJ0 *one* and the _AJ0 *one*

<u>Hits</u>: 3

Adjectival Modifiers in Elliptical Noun Phrases   109

Examples:

a. For me, a ladder has only <u>two rungs</u>—; **the bottom one** and **the top one**. (BNC, GXK 1045)

b. There are <u>two views of this task</u>, **the real one** and **the naive one**. (BNC, FNR 266)

c. On the seashore Kate threw <u>two balls</u> for the dogs, **the red one** and **the blue one**. (BNC, H7A 1820)

Indefinites

<u>Search string</u>: (a|an) _AJ0 *one* and (a|an) _AJ0 *one*

<u>Hits</u>: 5

Examples:

d. The 500C has <u>two ink cartridges</u> permanently installed; **a black one** and **a tri-colour one**. (BNC, FT8 1575)

e. My daddy has <u>two vans</u>, **a blue one** and **a yellow one**. (BNC, BNG 494)

f. There are <u>two forms of most UK mail addresses</u>, **a long one** and **a short one** (J1F 954)

g. It's only a problem for UK subscribers, most of whom automatically have a choice of <u>2 From: addresses</u>—**a long one** and **a short one**. (BNC, J1E 865)

h. He revealed that the reason for the subsidence was the presence of an underground pool where <u>two dragons</u> lived, **a red one** and **a white one**. (BNC, G2S 464)

(78) Coordination of two elliptical noun phrases (= C)

Definites

<u>Search string</u>: the _AJ0 and the _AJ0 "non-nominal element"[16] (see example 1c)

<u>Hits</u>: 31

Examples:

a. In every subject, scientific and non-scientific alike, there are <u>two possible approaches</u>, **the practical** and **the theoretical**. (BNC, ASY 696)

b. This strategy can be divided into <u>two approaches</u>, **the forceful** and **the logical**. (BNC, CEF 705)

110   *The Elliptical Noun Phrase in English*

    c. <u>The two dominant models</u> in discussion of the relationship are **the presidential** and **the parliamentary.** (BNC, GV5 567)

    d. Pull strategy can be divided up into <u>two approaches</u>, **the participative** and **the inspirational.** (BNC, CEF 841)

Indefinites
<u>Search string</u>: (alan) _AJ0 and (alan) _AJ0 "non-nominal element"
<u>Hits</u>: 0

(79) First conjunct bearing a lexical noun, the second containing *one* (= D)
Definites

<u>Search string</u>: the _AJ0 _NN1 and the _AJ0 *one*

<u>Hits</u>: 0

Indefinites
<u>Search string</u>: (alan) _AJ0 _NN1 and (alan) _AJ0 *one*
<u>Hits</u>: 0[17]

(80) First conjunct bearing no noun, the second containing *one* (= E)
Definites
<u>Search string</u>: the _AJ0 and the _AJ0 *one*
<u>Hits</u>: 0

Indefinites
<u>Search string</u>: (alan) _AJ0 and (alan) _AJ0 *one*
<u>Hits</u>: 0

Table 5.4 summarizes the findings. As becomes obvious, there is a strong preference for a silent noun in the Taxonomizing Construction. The version that contains a silent noun in each of the two conjuncts, search type C outlined in example (78), occurs 31 times and outranks all the other possible configurations.

There is an apparent mismatch at this point. In the analysis in Section 5.3.1.1, a total of 43 instances of this construction was identified, but here there are only 31. This derives from the additional search that included the most frequent adjectives tagged as common nouns, which added significantly to the results presented in Section 5.3.1.1. This strategy was not employed here. It would only have contributed to type C, the coordination of elliptical noun phrases, and this already features prominently among the results—no further evidence is needed here. The only other configuration comprising a

Adjectival Modifiers in Elliptical Noun Phrases   111

Table 5.4 Realization of nominal heads in Taxonomizing Constructions

Realization of the nominal head	Number of hits		
	Definite	Indefinite	Total
A) Lexical noun	8	4	12
B) *One*	3	5	8
C) Silent noun	31	0	31
D) Lexical noun and *one*	0	0	0
E) Silent noun and *one*	0	0	0

silent noun is the one outlined in example (80), type E,—here, an elliptical noun phrase would intervene between the antecedent noun phrase and the one that contains *one*. There are no hits for this, which suggests that a search for adjectives tagged as nouns in this context would have been redundant.

In consideration of the hypothesis this work started out with, that is, that noun ellipsis with adjectival modifiers is at best a marginal phenomenon in English, these results come as a surprise. A number of factors will be given consideration to explain this rather unexpected distribution.

5.4.2 Distance between Anaphor and Antecedent

One factor to be looked into is distance between anaphor and antecedent. This relates to the concept of mental accessibility as advocated, for example, in Ariel's (1990) highly influential work. This approach to the use of anaphoric forms will be discussed in more detail in Section 5.5, but for the present purpose, a brief summary suffices.

Ariel accounts for the use of referring expressions in terms of the degree of accessibility they encode. Speakers use different forms to instruct the addressee to locate given information by signaling how accessible it is to them. The degrees and their corresponding linguistic forms are illustrated in the "Accessibility Marking Scale" (Ariel 1990: 73), ranging from low accessibility markers (e.g., definite descriptions) to high accessibility markers (e.g., zero forms). It can be summarized in somewhat simpler terms: The more informative a form is and the larger its phonological size, the less accessible is its referent (see Ariel 2001). This can be transferred to N^0-anaphora—a repeated lexical noun contains most information (lexical contents, number, phonological form); hence it is the lowest accessibility marker. The silent noun conveys least information (no contents, no number, no phonological form) and thus represents the highest degree of accessibility. *One* occupies an intermediate position (no lexical contents, number, phonological form).

Ariel puts forth distance as one factor that determines accessibility of a referent. Since in the Taxonomizing Construction the anaphoric forms and their antecedents seem to be quite close at first sight, this aspect is analyzed here.

112 *The Elliptical Noun Phrase in English*

The distance was measured as follows: The counting starts with the first word following the antecedent; the modifier preceding the lexical noun, *one*, or the silent noun in the first conjunct is the last element that is factored in. Hence, in example (81), the distance is 8—*are, currently, being, investigated, these, are, the,* and *biological:*

(81) Two approaches are currently being investigated. These are ***the biological approach*** and ***the biochemical approach.*** (BNC, HSD 2025) (= example 76c)

Some instances of the empty type, C, were problematic to classify, because two nouns qualify as potential antecedents as in example (82).

(82) Traditionally, language teaching has divided discourse into two major categories, ***the spoken*** and ***the written,*** further divided into the four skills of speaking and listening, writing and reading. (BNC, F9W 1060)

In example (82) *discourse* was taken as the antecedent. This decision is based on the fact that *spoken* and *written* do not collocate with *category* in the BNC, whereas they do with *discourse*.[18] The distribution suggests that the silent noun is interpreted as referring back to *discourse*.

The results are presented in Table 5.5.

The data suggest that the lexical noun is repeated when the distance between antecedent and anaphor increases. However, the average value is biased due to two examples which display an exceptional large distance:

(83) It is already known that the normal reader has at his or her disposal two very different procedures (two very different sets of mental operations) for accomplishing the conversion of print to speech. These are now known as ***the lexical procedure*** and ***the nonlexical procedure.*** (BNC, HHY 7382) (= example 76d)

(84) A small wooden peg called a spile is knocked into the soft core of the shive. Two types are used: ***a soft spile*** and ***a hard spile.*** (BNC, A0A 122,3) (= example 76l)

Table 5.5 Distance between antecedent and nominal head

Nominal head	Number of hits	Average distance
A) Lexical noun	12	7.083(4.8)
B) *One*	8	3.75
C) Silent noun	31	4.839

Adjectival Modifiers in Elliptical Noun Phrases 113

The word distance in the former example is 22, and in the latter it is 15. If these are factored out, the average decreases to 4.8 words. Note that it equals the value for the silent noun, with an average distance of 4.839 words. Therefore, the choice between silent noun and lexical noun cannot be attributed to textual accessibility of referents. An even more unexpected outcome is the average for the use of *one*. Here, the value is lower than the one for the silent empty noun. Obviously, in this context, the use of noun ellipsis is determined by other factors (see subsection 5.5.2, which shows that distance plays a role in other contexts).

5.4.3 Text Types

Only one out of the 49 instances stems from the spoken component, that is, the Taxonomizing Construction appears to be a written-language phenomenon. Because discourse situations in written language might also contribute to the use of particular forms, text types were taken into consideration as well. The distribution of nominal forms across text types is illustrated in Table 5.6.

The majority of findings derive from academic and non-academic prose. This could imply that the use of noun ellipsis relates to the level of education of speaker and hearer. However, it should be kept in mind that this construction serves a categorizing function. The speaker creates taxonomies, where different subclasses are related to superordinate terms. Hence, it does not come as a surprise that the construction is found within these text types—research and science are the prime domains for establishing taxonomies. Non-academic prose here also comprises the fields natural science, social science, medicine, humanities and arts, as well as politics, law, and education, that is, further settings where classification is relevant. What is more, those instances where the lexical noun is repeated are to be found within the

Table 5.6 Taxonomizing Constructions across text types

Text Type	Nominal head			
	Lexical	*One*	Silent	Total
Written				
Academic prose	4	1	13	18
Non-academic prose	4	1	15	21
Fiction and verse	—	1	2	3
Other published written material	3	2	1	6
Unpublished written material	—	3	—	3
Spoken				
Other spoken material	1	—	—	1

114 *The Elliptical Noun Phrase in English*

same text types. Therefore, the explanation for the predominant use of the silent noun in these settings must be sought along different lines.

5.4.4 Antecedents of the Silent Noun and *One*

An aspect that has hitherto been neglected relates to the antecedent of the silent noun. Strikingly, the concepts that are categorized are mostly abstract rather than concrete. Abstract comprises thoughts, ideas, and concepts that lack a concrete realization such as *view, type, approach,* and *tradition.* Concrete refers to concepts that are realized in way that they can be perceived visually, audibly, and hapticly. This comprises *person, water,* and *van* from the above examples. The distinction, however, is by no means clear-cut. *Way* in the sense of *path* is something concrete, while it denotes an abstract concept in the example (85):

(85) We feel drawn to distinguish <u>two ways of knowing things</u>, *an inward way* and *an outward way.* (BNC, CK1 1288) (= example 76k)

Class (in the sense of social class) was difficult to classify because on the one hand it denotes people, that is, concrete entities, but on the other hand those people are classified according to a theoretical concept. The latter seemed to carry more weight in the following example. Therefore, *class* is treated as an abstract noun in the present case.

(86) <u>Three main classes</u>—*the upper class, the middle class,* and *the working class* will be considered in turn, though as will become clear, the location of the boundaries between these classes is disputed. (BNC, FB6 1454) (= example 76b)

The distribution of concrete and abstract antecedents is summarized in Table 5.7.

As the table displays, there are 39 instances of abstract antecedents, and only 12 antecedent nouns denote concrete entities. This is probably due to the context in which taxonomies are used. As argued above, the text types reflect that a classification of different types according to a distinguishing

Table 5.7 Antecedent types

Nominal Head	Antecedent	
	Concrete	Abstract
A) Lexical noun	2	10
B) *One*	7	1
C) Silent noun	3	28

Adjectival Modifiers in Elliptical Noun Phrases   115

property is frequently carried out within research and science. Hence, the distribution of abstract and concrete does not come unexpectedly. But the distribution displays some highly interesting aspects. While the repetition of a lexical noun and the use of the silent noun mostly display abstract concepts, the reference to concrete objects is accompanied by the use of *one*. Only a single instance of the antecedent denoting an abstract concept was found:

(87) There are <u>two views of this task,</u> *the real one* and *the naive one*.
      (BNC, FNR 266) (= example 77b)

The other nouns that function as antecedents for *one* are *ball, van, ink cartridge, address, rung*, and *dragon*.

It seems as if the use of *one* was dispreferred with an abstract entity rather than a concrete object as antecedent. This is not accounted for in the approaches discussed in Chapter 3 or in the one developed in Chapter 4. *One* was taken to be a functional element devoid of lexical content. It has repeatedly been emphasized that the only information it expresses is countability, number, and that an anaphoric relation holds. Countability was the only condition identified for its antecedent. Presumably, the reason for this rather unexpected distribution is that the interpretation of *one* as UNIT (or ENTITY) (see Llombart-Huesca 2002: 80), which arises because it is [+count], is perceived to be more compatible with concrete objects.

This has some important implications. If this is on the right track, the view of *one* as being completely devoid of lexical content needs to be reconsidered. Support for this derives from the distributional properties of *one*. As illustrated in Section 3.1, *one* readily allows for post-modifiers but not for complements.

(88) a. I met <u>the student from Germany</u> but I didn't meet **the *one*** from Italy.

      b. *<u>The destruction of Rome</u> was as cruel as **the *one*** of Carthage.

      c. *I met <u>the student of physics</u> but I didn't meet **the *one*** of chemistry. (Llombart-Huesca 2002: 65).

However, as Stirling and Huddleston remark, this depends on the type of noun as antecedent: "the inadmissible complements [. . .] are complements with the form of PPs, and the acceptability of complements of this kind depends on the nature of the antecedent noun" (2002: 1516). Role nouns (such as *boss* and *friend*), kinship nouns (e.g., *mother, father,* and *sister*), nouns denoting part-whole relationships (such as *cover, leg,* and *sleeve*), and agent nominalizations (e.g., *designer, student,* or *supporter*) do not allow for *one* being followed by a PP complement.

116 *The Elliptical Noun Phrase in English*

(89) a. Which <u>king</u> did you see? *The *one* of Belgium.

　　b. Which <u>sleeve</u> did you mend? *The *one* of the dress.
　　　(Stirling & Huddleston 2002: 1515)

Other nominal antecedents do allow for a PP complement as the following example illustrates:

(90) a. This <u>proof</u> of Taylor's theorem is better than **the *one* of Parzival's** inequality.

　　b. The <u>production</u> of Madame Butterfly was better than **the *one* of Tosca.**
　　　(Stirling & Huddleston 2002: 1515)

This demonstrates that *one* may well be dependent on the lexical meaning of the antecedent. However, even if this is on the right track, the use of a lexical or a silent noun for abstract interpretations has to be considered a preference rather than a grammatical requirement. As becomes clear in example (87), *one* is used with abstract nouns as antecedent. Still, this preference is one possible explanation for the rather unexpected distribution of nominal heads in these contexts.

5.4.5 Generic Reference

It was pointed out that Alexiadou and Gengel (forthcoming) ascribe the licensing of noun ellipsis with adjectives in French and English to the classifying properties of these adjectives. In subsection 5.3.2.1, I argued against the applicability of this notion to the phenomena under investigation here, but classification, although in a slightly different way, might still be relevant for the present approach. This relates to the discussion of the Human Construction. As observed in subsection 4.3.2.3, this construction, which always has the form definite article + adjective + silent noun, refers to an entire class rather than to individual entities. As soon as *one* is used, reference to individuals is licit. This parallels the situation in classifier languages where the generic reading is blocked once a classifier is used, which was taken as further evidence for an analogy between classification and the overt expression of number.

The Taxonomizing Construction does not refer to individuals either—Krifka et al. (1995) present the following examples of taxonomic noun phrases, which establish subkinds ("kind" is understood as denoting a class—genericity—in contrast to object reference—individuals).

(91) a. **One whale,** namely the blue whale, is nearly extinct.

　　b. **Two whales,** namely the blue whale and the fin whale, were put under protection.
　　　(Krifka et al. 1995: 74)

Adjectival Modifiers in Elliptical Noun Phrases   117

These constructions are reminiscent of the aforementioned cases, such as examples (92) and (93), where reference is made to two kinds of approach rather than to individuals.[19]

(92) This strategy can be divided into <u>two approaches</u>, **the forceful** and **the logical.** (BNC, CEF 705)

(93) One can identify <u>two broad types of approach</u>, which I will call **the democratic** and **the consultative.** (BNC, B2X 697–700) (= example 31)

Interestingly, when the noun phrases refer to individuals and not to an entire subclass, *one* is used. In example (94), there are certainly not two kinds of cars but rather two concrete instances of the car kind.

(94) My daddy has <u>two vans</u>, **a blue one** and **a yellow one.** (BNC, BNG 494) (= 77e)

Similarly, in example (95), there are two individual dragons, which happen to be red and white rather than a red and a white type of dragon.

(95) He revealed that the reason for the subsidence was the presence of an underground pool where <u>two dragons</u> lived, **a red one** and **a white one.** (BNC, G2S 464) (= 77h)

However, it has to be mentioned that in example (96), the two noun phrases containing *one* are construed with a generic reading.

(96) There are <u>two forms of most UK mail addresses</u>, **a long one** and **a short one** (BNC, J1F 954) (= example 77f)

Yet, even if this does not account for every case, this idea might explain why *one* is absent in the following examples.

(97) . . . and it is then that <u>whales</u> like **the blue** migrate towards the pole to feed. (BNC, AMS 929)

(98) The differences between these <u>two races of wild cat</u> support the idea that it was **the African** that originally gave rise to the domesticated feline. (BNC, BMG 1437)

118   *The Elliptical Noun Phrase in English*

5.5 ACCESSIBILITY

So far, the focus has been on the factors that allow for *one* to be left out. However, a second important question is why *one* is left out (provided it is licit, of course). In subsection 5.4.3, this was briefly touched upon when the concept of accessibility was mentioned.

The accessibility approach to the use of anaphoric forms is based on the idea that speakers indicate the statuses antecedents have in the hearer's memory, in order to make the retrieval of that information easier for them. Ariel (1990, 2001) presents the following Accessibility Scale, which shows the gradient of accessibility encoded in anaphoric forms, proceeding from low to high accessibility.

(99) Full name + modifier > full name > long definite description > short definite description > last name > first name > distal demonstrative + modifier > proximate demonstrative + modifier > distal demonstrative + NP > proximate demonstrative + NP > distal demonstrative (-NP) > proximate demonstrative (-NP) > stressed pronoun + gesture > stressed pronoun > unstressed pronoun > clitized pronoun > verbal person inflections > zero (Ariel 2001: 31)

This concept was chosen for the present purpose because it does away with the notion of "givenness." which is not applicable to empty nouns because anaphora obtains below the phrase level, that is, referents are not given or known. As laid out in detail in Section 4.1, noun phrases containing a silent noun or *one* are usually not coreferential to those containing the antecedent nouns. Thus, even though the noun phrase contains an anaphoric form, it introduces a new referent.[20] As mentioned before, the idea that the more information an anaphoric expression conveys, the less accessible its antecedent is can be applied to N-anaphora as well. This gives rise to the following cline, proceeding from low to high accessibility.

(100) lexical noun > overt empty noun *one* > silent empty noun

The analysis in the previous section suggests that the distribution of empty forms in the Taxonomizing Construction is subject to factors other than accessibility, but there are contexts where the status of referents arguably leads to the use of a silent noun. The first was identified in the data from the spoken component, where the antecedents are situationally accessible. In example (11), presented in Section 5.2, the conversation centers on beads of different colors, and the probability of drawing a particular bead from a bag. This means the referents are not only physically present in the text-external world, they also constitute the discourse topic. This salience, according to Ariel (1990), results in high accessibility.

Adjectival Modifiers in Elliptical Noun Phrases 119

Furthermore, entities can be inferentially accessible. They show different degrees of accessibility depending on the cost of the inference that is required. An important cognitive concept to be mentioned here is the frame (or schema) proposed by Fillmore (1976, 1982). A frame is defined as a system of related concepts—in order to understand one of those concepts the whole structure has to be understood. Similarly, if one concept is used within the discourse, the concepts it is related to become active as well. Frame-inducing entities are more accessible than those not related to a specific frame (Ariel 2001). This can account for examples such as the following:

(101) Slave masters matched their <u>gladiators</u> and rewarded **the successful** with relief from plantation duties, the possibility of travel and, ultimately, freedom. (BNC, CL1 460)

In example (101), the frame is a match and because of his or her world knowledge the hearer knows that, in competitive contexts, there are successful and unsuccessful participants. Therefore, in some contexts, the speaker may indicate that the referent is highly accessible with the help of an elliptical noun phrase, because he or she expects the hearer to make out the individual in question on the basis of world knowledge.

The above indicates that an analysis of head noun variation in terms of accessibility might prove fruitful, even if no viable results were yielded in terms of taxonomies. In what follows, a context that readily allows for the use of both empty nouns will be under consideration.

5.5.1 Anaphoric Head Noun Realizations with *Old* and *New*

In order to find a basis on which the use of the three possible heads (lexical, *one*, silent) can be compared, noun phrases containing *new* and *old* were analyzed. These two adjectives were chosen because they feature prominently as modifiers of silent nouns (the first search yielded 68 hits for *new* and 109 for *old*). Furthermore, in the majority of cases the other one of the pair was found in the context as well. Two modifiers were taken to make sure that there are (at least) two referents in the context. A number of facts justifies the restriction of this search to these two modifiers. First and foremost, this search also implies a manual analysis of the data—the cases to be excluded are outlined below (example 103)—therefore, the search had to be restricted to a manageable portion of examples. Second, the frequent use of *old* and *new* with noun ellipsis suggests that a sufficient number of results to provide a basis for comparison can be found.

In order to restrict the search for contexts that include *old* and *new* at the same time, the sentence was chosen as a boundary. This is a quite pretheoretical term based on punctuation means rather than on syntactic considerations (the full stop serves as a marker here), but it is useful because many

120   *The Elliptical Noun Phrase in English*

of the above examples showed that *old* and *new* often co-occur within a complex clause:

(102) Because the innovator has for enemies all those who have done well under the old conditions . . . and lukewarm defenders in those who may do well under **the new.** (BNC, CKS 169) (= example 41a)

For this reason, the sentence was chosen as boundary.

The search for *new* <<s>> *old* yielded 3535 hits. POS tags were not used here because, as explained above, tagging is not reliable in a search for silent categories. The 3535 hits were sorted according to the following aspects:

(103) Exclusion of certain configurations

a. Nonattributive (i.e., predicative) use of the modifiers:

Example: If Bell is ruled out as too **old** and Ramsey as too **new,** who else has stature? (BNC, A68 2127)

b. Prenominal coordination of modifiers:

Example: The Government is as keen as anyone else to ensure that this fine collection of **old and new varieties** is maintained to a high standard. (BNC, A4U 413)

c. *Old* or *new* as post-modifier:

Example: Jackson quotes Freud's view that something has to be added to what is novel and unfamiliar to make it uncanny; this something is "nothing **new** or alien, but something which is familiar and **old**—established in the mind and become alienated from it through the process of repression" (p. 66). (BNC, A6D 1384)

d. The Human Construction:

Example: How can the erotic stirring for Aeneas be "**new,**" when it is explicitly saturated with sentiment for **the old,** the dead, for "Sicheus"? (BNC, A1B 1237)

e. The Abstract Construction:

Example: Nice echo too of medieval stained glass, while helping to establish principle of making **the utterly new** out of **the old,** the ordinary, the commonplace—what could be more ordinary than fuse-wire? (BNC, A08 1542)

f. Modifier as part of a proper name:

Example: He was due to join up with **his old friend** Irving Layton again, and former professor F. R. Scott at **New York's** prestigious YM/YWCA centre on 92nd Street. (BNC, A0P 1628)

Adjectival Modifiers in Elliptical Noun Phrases 121

(104) Use of two different lexical nouns with *new* and *old*

    a. In **the new battle** against inflation, **the old claim** that there is no alternative has started to sound out of date. (BNC, A5K 39)

    b. Its answers to **new problems** tend to be **old answers**—answers which have answered other questions in the past, and which will answer other questions in the future. (BNC, ASD 616)

(105) Use of a silent noun with *old,* with *new,* or with both modifiers

    a. The lower substage of barbarism is common and is marked by the discovery of pottery, but the middle substage is marked by agriculture and the domestication of plants in <u>the new world,</u> and by pastoralism and the domestication of animals in **the old.** (BNC, A6S 686)

    b. Richard Rogers has adopted a high-tech approach, carefully distinguishing between <u>the old work</u> and **the new.** (BNC, AR9 1808)

(106) Use of *one*-insertion with *old,* with *new* or with both modifiers

    a. For example, some have difficulties in retrieving semantic information about people (for example their occupation), some have difficulties specific to the retrieval of people's names, and some can remember <u>old faces</u> but cannot learn **new ones.** (BNC, A0T 1201)

    b. <u>The old Union station</u> had been in a rambling neo-Romanesque style, but **the new one** was to match the grandest of the American Beaux-Arts school, and in some ways surpass them. (BNC, AR0 1048)

(107) Repetition of the lexical noun with *new* and *old*

    a. Then <u>new gravel</u> is laid directly on top—**the old gravel** will form a firm foundation. (BNC, A16 1782)

    b. <u>All this new history</u> makes **old history** even more important. (BNC, A2W 125)

The results are summarized in Table 5.8. The total number of hits is 3535; 997 instances fall into the categories displayed in example (103) and thus were excluded. This renders a total of 2538 hits for *old* and *new* as nominal premodifiers (lexical, *one,* or silent noun) within one sentence. This number is further divided into the use of different lexical nouns (1437 instances), the repetition of the same noun with *old* and *new* (383 hits), the use of *one*-insertion with one or both of the modifiers (450 instances), and the use of the silent noun with *one* or both of the modifiers[21] (268 hits).

Note that there are instances among the use of a silent noun within this context that were not covered by the first search, as the latter does not include

122 *The Elliptical Noun Phrase in English*

Table 5.8 Old and *new* as nominal modifiers

Noun modified by *old* and *new*	Number of hits
Old and *new* as nominal modifiers	2538
Use of two different lexical nouns	1437
Repetition of the lexical noun	383
One	450
Silent noun	268

cases of an elliptical noun phrase without a determiner (or a numeral). Interestingly, some of these instances were identified in this analysis:

(108) a. He replaced floors, fallen plaster, mended the machineries of lavatory cisterns and, borrowing the car from next door, got <u>new piping</u> to replace **old.** (BNC, EV1 1593)

  b. They could see the patchwork of <u>new fabric</u> over **old,** where the repairs hadn't been painted yet. (BNC, HRA 2365)

(109) Replacing <u>new genes</u> for **old**—homologous recombination—is now feasible in animal cells, but the technology requires a great deal of refinement before such a feat could be achieved in human somatic cells. (BNC, FT3 50)

As shown in the examples, an adjective can occur as modifier of a silent noun even when there is no determiner. This holds for both mass interpretations (example 108) and count interpretations (example 109).

There are two aspects of the search that require further elaboration. First of all, in light of the assumption that noun ellipsis with adjectival remnants in English is a marginal phenomenon at best, the amount of hits for noun ellipsis in the *old-new* context is somewhat surprising—the elliptical cases make up almost a quarter of the total (24.34 percent). Hence, noun ellipsis with adjectival remnants can hardly be considered marginal in English. The second aspect concerns the distribution of the different configurations. Note that this does not come unexpectedly: *One*-insertion is preferred to both a silent noun and to the repetition of the lexical noun, with the latter still outranking the use of the silent noun in terms of frequency. Still, the question remains as to whether any patterns governing the choice of nominal head realization (lexical, *one,* silent) can be identified.

Before the analysis can be carried out, the results need further refinement in order to exclude data that might bias the analysis. There are three aspects to be addressed: mass interpretations, proper nouns, and number disambiguation.

Adjectival Modifiers in Elliptical Noun Phrases 123

It has been pointed out throughout this work that *one* cannot be used in mass noun phrases, which reduces the choice of nominal forms to two (silent and lexical noun). For this reason, examples such as the following were factored out.

(110) But we used to turn it over, not like they push it in front, <u>new stuff</u> in front of **old,** we never had that, we never did that. (BNC, HF3 701)

(111) They're useful in surgery to keep blood flowing at the right speed and sucking <u>old blood</u> from re-attached parts so **new blood** flows in quickly. (BNC, ARJ 894)

The second point pertains to examples such as the following, where *old* and *new* are parts of complex proper nouns. These were excluded as well.

(112) There is much about the love and forgiveness of God in <u>the Old Testament</u>, and much about his righteous anger and judgement in **the New.** (BNC, EFT 487)

(113) In this latter sense, preachers and theologians sought in <u>the Old Testament</u> (with its sometimes unedifying stories) types of the characters in **the New Testament.** (BNC, GU7 57)

Another aspect relates to *one* as a means to disambiguate number. As example (114) shows, antecedent phrase and anaphoric phrase do not necessarily match in number. The mismatch is indicated by *one*—because the anaphoric phrase is definite, number can only be conveyed by an overt noun.

(114) I am afraid the above formulae are wrong because <u>our new solenoids</u> don't look the same as **the old one.** BNC, FEF 1181

In example (115), in contrast, there is no indication whether the elliptical noun phrase is singular or plural.

(115) And they may need to pay more if enough workers are to be available—unless <u>sufficient old machines</u> are forced out of operation there will be a shortage of workers to operate **the new.** (BNC, K8U 128)

More context is needed to determine the number properties of the elliptical noun phrase.

For this reason, definite noun phrases were factored out as well, and the analysis was restricted to indefinite plural count noun phrases. An example for each of the three heads is provided.

(116) <u>Many old friends</u> had been greeted and **new friends** made. (BNC, CRJ 396)

124   *The Elliptical Noun Phrase in English*

(117) She has to decide, as she goes, how and when to weave in <u>new strands</u> and drop **old ones,** still keeping the continuity of design. (BNC, CCN 580)

(118) In the meantime the highest costs of these changes are borne by those made redundant as <u>new technologies</u> replace **old.** (BNC, CAN 228)

The subset of data created on the basis of the above condition contains 41 instances of a repeated lexical head, 129 instances of *one*-insertion, and 27 instances of elliptical noun phrases.

5.5.2 Factors Determining Accessibility

According to Ariel (1990, 2001), accessibility is determined by a range of different aspects, such as distance, competition of antecedents, syntactic role of antecedents (subjects are more accessible than nonsubjects), and saliency. The first factor taken into consideration is the distance between antecedent and anaphora measured in words, as described in subsection 5.4.2.

The number of instances per distance value for each type of head is presented in Figure 5.1. As can be seen from the diagram, elliptical noun phrases are only used for the shorter distances, the largest being eight words. Anaphoric relations with lexical heads, on the other hand, can cross greater

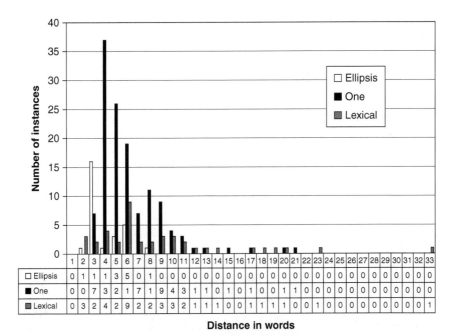

Figure 5.1 Distance between anaphor and antecedent.

Adjectival Modifiers in Elliptical Noun Phrases 125

distances, amounting to 33 words. As expected, *one* can be found in an intermediate position. The mean distance for lexical nouns is 9 words, for *one* it is 6.2 and for the silent noun it is 4, which is statistically significant.[22]

Because it is clear that distance is the main factor in this context, other factors will only be discussed very briefly, in order to show how this ties in with the above findings.

An aspect that leads to a decrease in accessibility is competition on the role of antecedent: If there are elements between antecedent and anaphor that qualify as potential antecedents, lower accessibility markers are used. Example (119) is one of the repetition of the lexical noun with lots of intervening nominal elements:

(119) <u>The old distributaries</u> may still be frozen and incapable of handling the volume of the river and the load it is carrying, so that there is wholesale bank breaching, flooding, and the creation of **new distributaries.** (BNC, GV0 855)

If an element containing less information than a lexical noun was used here, the structure would be very hard to process. This, of course, also corresponds to distance: The greater the distance, the more likely it is to have competing nominal expressions.

More interesting insights can be derived from cases where distance does not correspond to the anaphoric element that is used, as in the example of the greatest distance between antecedent and ellipsis site. What is striking is the complexity of the antecedent *old peoples and old cultures*. Using a lexical element here would imply the repetition of a lot of redundant material within a relatively short range, which is why a silent form is used.

(120) His reply to the expected criticism is that ideals must be striven for particularly now since "in a position in which <u>old peoples and old cultures</u> are likely to be supplanted by **new**—we are in a common danger to all races over the whole circumference of the globe." (BNC, A6B 2094)

However, I have no answer why this is the elliptical form and not *one*, because *one* can be used with complex antecedents, as example (121) illustrates.

(121) The furniture was on the move too, with <u>the old, solid benches and wooden chairs</u> being replaced with **curving, light-weight new ones** in bright colours. (BNC, K8V 3614)

Further examples of the use of silent nouns after greater distances show antecedents in subject position. According to Ariel (2001), this position leads to higher accessibility of the antecedents.

126 *The Elliptical Noun Phrase in English*

(122) And <u>old centres</u> expanded as rapidly as **new.** (BNC, EA7 594)

(123) <u>Old myths</u> are, however, replaced by **new** as the combination of modern technology . . . (BNC, ADD 1208)

(124) <u>New sets</u> can be made from **old** in several ways, one of which we saw above in defining Z+ in terms of Z. (BNC, EV9365)

Another interesting case is a short distance for lexical nouns. In example (125), two noun phrases with the same lexical head are adjacent to each other.

(125) But he could be touchpaper, and a spark from a fancied slight, a disagreement over politics, a moment of heedlessness from someone, and he would catch and soon the conflagration was at full blast consuming everything in its path: <u>new friendships</u>, **old friendships,** new clients, his reputation, his wife's love, even that. (BNC, G0S 2021)

This apparent violation of the accessibility criterion serves a stylistic purpose: The redundant repetition of the lexical head in the enumeration underlines the abundance of things falling victim to the protagonist's temper, that is, the violation of the accessibility criterion has a pragmatic effect. This shows that even if distance is the main aspect, the other cases can be accounted for as well.

5.6 SUMMARY AND CONCLUSION

The corpus analysis revealed that noun ellipsis with adjectival modifiers is licit in English. In the main analysis, 965 elliptical noun phrases were identified; two subsequent studies added further findings. It is not just that these phrases are licit, the analysis of head noun realization with *old* and *new* suggests that the phenomenon is not even as marginal as expected. The discussion of various aspects demonstrated that noun ellipsis with adjectives is not a uniform phenomenon, that is, it is not predictable on the basis of a single factor. The aspects taken into account mainly fall into two groups: explanations for why *one* is not required, and motivations for the use of a silent empty noun.

The first distinction that had to be made pertains to spoken and written language and the discourse situation. In terms of spoken language, several contexts were identified where the referents under consideration are highly salient due to their being discourse topics and their presence in the text-external world. The analysis showed that mainly adjectives denoting basic notions (see Payne & Huddleston 2002) are used in these contexts. This is because in terms of situationally accessible referents, clearly identifiable properties inherent to an object such as color allow for individuation more

Adjectival Modifiers in Elliptical Noun Phrases 127

easily than speaker-oriented properties such as those expressed by adjectives of value.

In terms of written language, the adjectives used in elliptical noun phrases did not mirror the pattern identified for the spoken data. In order to account for the distribution of noun ellipsis, first nonpragmatic factors were taken into consideration. In some cases, *one* cannot be used, which reduces the choice of possible head realizations to two (lexical and silent). This holds for cases where the antecedent phrase is non-count and for those where the antecedent is part of a complex proper noun such as *the Old Testament*.

Some more tentative proposals were made with respect to genericity and types of antecedent. This relates to what has been called Taxonomizing Construction—a construction that displays a preference for noun ellipsis. One possible explanation is that generic noun phrases in taxonomies, that is, where reference is made to subkinds, are dispreferred with an overt empty noun due to the classification properties of number on *one*. Another observation was that *one* is only used when the phrases refer to concrete (rather than abstract) entities—however, this coincides with them being used nongenerically, and, hence, more research is needed to isolate the relevant factor. It also has to be pointed out that none of the two criteria are absolute—there are taxonomic contexts that display *one*-insertion and cases of *one*-insertion with abstract antecedents.

A further aspect discussed was the contextual limitation of sets of referents. In the Taxonomizing Construction, the cardinality of the set is indicated, and the referents are exhaustively identified. Arguably, a similar mechanism applies in terms of binary pairs of adjectives, which imply duality of the set of referents. This contextual limitation allows for individuals to be identified. Because identifiability of an entity implies that its mass-count properties are identifiable as well, *one* can be left out here. Furthermore, if a referent is clearly identifiable, it is linked to the antecedent, and, hence, the noun phrase is clearly prevented from receiving an interpretation as [+human] or [+abstract].

In addition to the question of why *one* can be left out (or why it has to be left out), the question of why it *is* omitted was discussed. This aspect was addressed in a study of head noun realizations. It was argued that the concept of accessibility can be applied to the phenomenon under consideration, even though only the noun and not the entire noun phrase is anaphoric. The repeated lexical noun was regarded as a low accessibility marker, *one* was considered an intermediate marker, and the silent noun was taken as encoding high accessibility. This was related to the semantic, morphological, and phonological properties of the items; the lexical noun is deaccented but bears lexical meaning, *one* is deaccented and is semantically empty, and the silent noun is devoid of lexical meaning as well and has undergone the strongest possible form of phonological attenuation, that is, deletion (see Lambrecht 1994). The analysis revealed that distance between anaphor and antecedent is the most important factor: Elliptical noun phrases are used

128   *The Elliptical Noun Phrase in English*

with the shortest distance, lexical nouns with the longest. Apparent violations of the proper coding of accessibility were argued to serve particular stylistic purposes.

The corpus analysis illustrated that noun ellipsis with adjectival modifiers cannot be accounted for by one single concept only; rather, a range of different factors have to be taken into consideration. The notion of contrast or contrastive context as adhered to in the literature is much too vague to account for the use of elliptical noun phrases. I hope to have shown that it can be broken up into more fine-grained distinctions to provide a more thorough account for the complexities of the phenomenon.

6 Summary

This study explored the structure and aspects of the use of the elliptical noun phrase in English. The aim of this study was twofold. First, it attempted to account for the structure of elliptical noun phrases in English in general. Second, it analyzed the (pragmatic) conditions on noun ellipsis with adjectival modifiers, an aspect that has not received too much attention in the literature.

Several types of noun phrases that lack lexical heads had to be distinguished (see Chapter 1):

(1) Noun ellipsis

While Kim had lots of <u>books</u>, Pat had **very few.**

(2) *One*-insertion

I asked for a <u>key</u> but he gave me the wrong **one.**

(3) The partitive construction

Few of her <u>friends</u> knew she was ill.

(4) The Human Construction

The rich cannot enter the kingdom of Heaven.

(5) The Abstract Construction

We are going to attempt **the utterly impossible.**

These constructions all contain a (semantically) empty noun, but the focus of this work was on the first two, which are interpreted via an antecedent in the (extra-) linguistic context. Even though the above constructions are closely related, in particular the parallels between noun ellipsis and *one*-insertion are overlooked in many accounts for noun ellipsis, as outlined in Chapter 3. This gives rise to empirical and theoretical problems that the present work attempted to resolve.

One and the silent noun share a range of properties. First, both are anaphoric, that is, descriptively empty and hence dependent on an antecedent. If this antecedent is absent, an interpretation as [+human] arises (in

130 *The Elliptical Noun Phrase in English*

addition, the silent noun also allows for [+abstract] interpretations, as it is not restricted to count noun phrases). Both elements are subject to the same semantico-pragmatic principles, summarized as the contrast condition. On a syntactic level, they also display the same properties. Both readily allow for, but generally do not license, complements. On the basis of these insights, it was concluded that *one* is the overt form of a silent empty noun (see also Panagiotidis 2003a, b).

The licensing conditions on both empty nouns were laid out in detail in Chapter 4. The first was the so-called contrast (or non-identity) condition, which pertains to the relations between the noun phrase providing the antecedent and the one hosting the anaphoric noun. Three different types were identified (see Günther 2011): (a) partitive relations, where the referent of the anaphoric phrase is included in the set denoted by the antecedent phrase (example 6), (b) the referents of the two phrases are members of the same class (denoted by the antecedent noun) (example 7), and (c), referential identity with contrast obtaining on the lexical level (example 8).

(6) A narrow path led between <u>the two waters,</u> **the wild** and **the domesticated.** (BNC, ADM 409)

(7) They are trying to isolate <u>their good properties</u> from **the bad.** (BNC, AKL 309)

(8) <u>His hand,</u> **the same one he injured in April last year,** needs at least two weeks' rest, but he should be back in the ring in February. (BNC, A99)

In the next step, the relation between *one* and silent noun was analyzed in order to account for the licensing of noun ellipsis. The difference between the two can be summarized as follows: *One* has a phonological form, it hosts number morphology, and thus is a count noun, whereas the silent noun is compatible with mass readings as well. A further difference displays in terms of elements that precede the nouns. They fall into three categories: those that require *one*, those that cannot take *one*, and finally those that can occur with both forms. It was observed that a specification with regard to countability determines the form of the noun: Elements that are [-count] always need a silent noun, and those that are unspecified need *one*. It was suggested that the empty noun remains silent if the preceding element already expresses the relevant features, because in that case an overt form would be redundant. If an unspecified element such as a property-denoting adjective intervenes, *one* becomes visible. This process of deletion under adjacency puts the focus on linearity rather than locating a licensing mechanism in the syntax.

Although the findings are fully compatible with a traditional account of the noun phrase and countability, they were integrated into a nominal classification approach with the underlying assumption that the mass-count distinction is structurally represented. Count noun phrases have a separate functional projection for number, whereas mass noun phrases do not (as, e.g., argued by Borer 2005). Number thus plays a role in the mass-count distinction and is comparable to numeral classifiers in the classifier languages. The idea put forth in this work is that the empty noun surfaces as *one* as soon as it combines with number morphology—a view in which *one* is endowed with classifier-like properties. The advantages of this approach are that parallels to classifier languages can be captured: Classifiers can be used anaphorically. Furthermore, the silent noun that occurs in the Human Construction can be explained: As soon as *one* is used, reference can be made to individuals, that is, the phrase does not necessarily denote the entire class. Similarly, the use of classifiers is not licit in generic noun phrases in classifier languages.

In a next step, the analysis was extended to noun ellipsis in German. It was argued that gender is the corresponding noun categorization device, expressed through adjectival inflection. Apparent inflectional suffixes that only display in elliptical noun phrases were considered as morphologically bound pronouns, comparable to English *one* (see Corver & van Koppen 2011).

The second part of the book dealt with the use of elliptical noun phrases with adjectival modifiers. The point of departure was the question if a particular type of adjectival modifier allows for a silent noun (as claimed by Payne & Huddleston 2002), or whether the use of noun ellipsis with adjectival modifiers is determined by contrastiveness of the contexts, as often observed in the literature. For this purpose, three analyses of the British National Corpus were conducted.

The first study showed that noun ellipsis in English is licit with adjectival modifiers: 965 instances of elliptical noun phrases were identified. With regard to spoken language data, Payne and Huddleston's claim was confirmed: Adjectives denoting basic properties (such as color) occur quite frequently, arguably because they allow for the identification of referents more easily than more speaker-oriented notions. However, the data from the written component did not mirror this distribution, which required closer scrutiny of the contexts in which the noun phrases occur.

The first factor that was identified relates to the identification of referents that stem from contextually limited sets. This was evident in taxonomies where the cardinality of the set was explicitly mentioned as well as in cases of modifiers that form binary pairs and thus imply a duality of the set.

Further factors emerged in two follow-up studies on the Taxonomizing Construction, and the realization of the nominal head with the modifiers *old* and *new*. Taxonomies revealed a preference for silent nouns, which was attributed to two possible factors: abstract antecedents and reference to subkinds. It was suggested that the unit meaning of *one* is possibly more difficult to conceptualize with abstract antecedents. However, even if this (highly tentative) proposal is on the right track, it is not an absolute condition but merely a preference. The second aspect that was discussed, generic reference to subclasses, is not absolute either, as counterexamples illustrate.

132 *The Elliptical Noun Phrase in English*

A further point that was tested, the distance between anaphoric form and antecedent, did not play a role in this context. However, distance turned out to be crucial in other contexts, as indicated by a subsequent study on head noun realizations with the modifiers *old* and *new*. The latter analysis first demonstrated that a thorough refinement of the data was necessary to yield a basis of comparison, because in many cases, the choices between heads are reduced to two, because *one* is excluded (as, e.g., with mass antecedents). Therefore, undetermined plural noun phrases were examined with respect to factors that determine the nominal form. The data were accounted for with the help accessibility theory: Speakers use different nominal forms to signal how accessible an item is to the hearer, that is, which status it has in the hearer's memory. A silent noun corresponds to a referent being highly accessible because it contains no information; a repeated lexical noun encodes low accessibility because it conveys most information, while *one* signals medium accessibility. As the coding of accessibility is a complex matter and subject to a variety of interacting factors, a number of aspects were discussed. In the present case, distance between anaphor and antecedent fully accounts for the data: Noun ellipsis is used with shorter distances. Outliers were shown to also be compatible with the analysis: Topics are, according to Ariel (1990, 2001), more accessible than nontopics, which explains the cases of longer distances for silent nouns. Furthermore, apparent violations of the accessibility marking scale, such as the use of a repeated lexical noun within a short distance, were argued to serve pragmatic functions.

The analysis illustrated, I believe, that noun ellipsis with adjectival modifiers in English is a complex phenomenon, which cannot be accounted for by broad and vague concepts such as contrastiveness or salient contexts. Rather, more fined-grained, distinct notions need to be applied, in order to provide a satisfying account for the pragmatics of noun ellipsis in English. I hope to have shown that a thorough analysis of the phenomenon hitherto classified as marginal is highly relevant for linguistic analysis, because it provides deeper insights into how pragmatic principles interact with structural properties of the noun phrase.

Notes

NOTES TO CHAPTER 1

1. *One* is considered to be a noun devoid of lexical meaning; see Section 3.1 for a detailed discussion.
2. In the literature, the term *one*-anaphora is used as well (see, e.g., Dahl 1985).
3. The use of adjectives in the Human and the Abstract Constructions, that is, the non–antecedent-based nounless noun phrases, is generally not subject to discussion. As Borer and Roy (2010) point out, these constructions are fully productive (but see Giannakidou & Stavrou 1999 for the opposite claim).
4. For detailed information, the reader is referred to Hoffmann et al. 2008, and the BNC website http://www.natcorp.ox.ac.uk/corpus/index.xml.
5. This corpus is accessible online at http://corpus.byu.edu/coca/.
6. For detailed information on the corpus and its sub-corpora, see http://www.ids-mannheim.de/kl/projekte/korpora/archiv.html.

NOTES TO CHAPTER 2

1. As will be argued in Chapter 4, *one*-insertion is only licit if the noun phrase is interpreted as [+count]. This also indicates that the choice between noun ellipsis and *one*-insertion (or between noun ellipsis and the repetition of the lexical material expressed in the antecedent—a choice that is governed by pragmatic factors; see Chapter 5) is determined by the antecedent as well. When the latter receives a mass interpretation, *one*-insertion is not possible. Example (i) shows that if the noun phrase containing the antecedent is mass (such as *advice*), the elliptical phrase cannot take *one* (see also Dahl 1985: 8; Kester 1996b: 268):
   (i) *The advice you gave was more useful than the one I received from the Dean. (Stirling & Huddleston 2002: 1515)
   For a detailed discussion of the properties of *one* and its function the reader is referred to Chapter 4.
2. Note that these examples differ from those provided by Payne and Huddleston in two ways. In the first example, *tea* is used as a mass noun in this context. Thus, it is not compatible with *one*, as shown in (ii). Therefore, the only way to use an overt nominal in this context is to repeat the lexical noun, as illustrated in (iii).
   (i) I like strong tea.
   (ii) *I suppose weak one is better for you.
   (iii) I suppose weak tea is better for you.

134 *Notes*

The second example provided by Bouchard, example (15), differs from those outlined in subsection 2.1.2 in that the modifier that occurs in the elliptical NP, *straight,* is repeated, that is, the noun phrase is not introducing a new referent, in contrast to the noun phrases in the aforementioned examples.

For a detailed discussion of the role of contextual factors in noun ellipsis phenomena, see Chapter 5. The interaction of contrast and (co-)reference with noun ellipsis is accounted for in Section 4.1.

3. For an overview of German parts of speech and their morphosyntactic properties, see Zifonun et al. (1997: 21–67); for an extensive description of the structure of the German noun phrase, see ibid. (1926–2072).

4. In traditional German grammars, a further category, mixed inflection, is applied to cases where elements display both forms in their paradigms.

5. The well-known fact that adjectives are subject to certain (universal) ordering restrictions has been discussed extensively in the literature. For English, which only allows for stacked adjectival modification in prenominal position, this adjectival order naturally only affects the premodifying string. However, it has been claimed for other languages that the adjectives are ordered relative to their distance to the head noun. Thus, they do not necessarily have to occur in prenominal position. For an overview the reader is referred to Dixon (1982), Scott (2002), and Sproat and Shih (1991).

NOTES TO CHAPTER 3

1. That is, except for the singular indefinite article, *a,* which takes neither of the two forms.

2. It should be emphasized that there are, of course, different types of *one.* The antecedent-bound dummy *one* (often labeled pronominal *one*; see Stirling & Huddleston 2002, but note that Payne & Huddleston 2002 consider it to be a count noun) has to be distinguished from a non–antecedent-bound third person singular pronoun *one,* which is used nonreferentially to talk about groups of people (Payne & Huddleston 2002: 426f).

   (i) One shouldn't take oneself too seriously.
   (ii) One can't be too careful in these matters, can one?(Payne & Huddleston 2002: 426)

   In addition, *one* can be used as a cardinal numeral, either in contrast with higher cardinal numerals (iii) or as a kind of stressed counterpart of the indefinite article (iv):

   (iii) We have one son and two daughters.
   (iv) Not one student failed.(ibid.)

3. As Payne and Huddleston (2002) point out, *one* can sometimes be followed by a complement, depending on the type of antecedent (see also Section 5.4.4).

4. See also Corver and van Koppen (2011: note 4), where the empty noun's inability to select complements is accounted for in terms of their inability to assign θ-roles.

5. For a concise summary of the history of *pro,* see Panagiotidis (2003a) and references therein.

6. A number projection dominating NP was first proposed by Ritter (1991) for Hebrew. Lobeck adopts her analysis, arguing that indefinite noun phrases are headed by Num, and definite noun phrases are DPs (Lobeck 1995: Chapter 3).

7. Note that this schwa ending is not always considered an inflectional suffix. Corver and van Koppen (2009) take the *-e* to be an inflectional ending that can function as a focus marker at the same time (see Section 2.2.3). In their

Notes 135

2011 paper, however, they propose that it is a weak pronominal with bound morphemic status functioning as head in noun ellipsis contexts (Corver & van Koppen 2011).

8. López (2000) proposes, "elided constituents are licensed when they are associated with a discourse-linking functional category" (2000: 187). The notion of D-linking was introduced by Pesetsky (1987) for *wh*- words, which are able to pick a referent from a set that is contextually accessible to both speaker and hearer. Hence, discourse-linking elements imply the existence of a superset from which the referent is picked out. This implication of a set-relation is very closely related to the notion of partitivity as López remarks (2000: note 11). Enç (1991) conflates the two notions.

9. Note that this definition of "classifying" is extremely vague—what counts as classifying is highly speaker dependent because the classifying adjective constitutes a pragmatic category.

10. There are 46 instances of *every single one of* in the BNC. Two examples are:
    (i) Those five gates of hell, he'd be put through **every single one of them.** (C86 1000)
    (ii) She looked **at every single one of the hundreds of photos** and couldn't stop smiling at the memory. (CEK 3649)

11. I am thankful to Renate Musan for a useful hint.

12. *One* is taken into account here as well, because it is subject to the same semantic conditions as noun ellipsis (see Section 3.1 and the analysis in Chapter 4).

13. This is contrary to van Hoof 2005, who claims that only intersective adjectives allow for noun ellipsis. Eguren (2010: 449) provides an example from Spanish, which also corroborates the fact that nonintersective modifiers are licit in elliptical noun phrases:
    (i) El juez condenó al verdadero asesino y al presunto __.
    "The judge found both the true murderer and the alleged murderer guilty."
    The phenomenon is also attested to in German, as shown by the following data.
    (ii) Bei Anzeichen einer Bedrohung sind die echten Gefahren nicht immer von **den vermeintlichen** zu unterscheiden.
    "When a threat is faced, the real dangers are not always distinguishable from the alleged ones." (DPA09/MAR.06138)
    (iii) Für mich als Verbraucher ist dieser Fortschritt nur **ein vermeintlicher,** denn ich brauche ihn nicht.
    'For me as a consumer, this progress is only an apparent one, for I don't need it.' (DPA09/APR.07108)

14. In spoken language, these potential ambiguities are resolved by prosody.

15. Interestingly, Bouchard considers the phrasal genitive to be partitive because "a possessor always implies a contextually active superset which the possessed object is picked out of" (2002: 224). However, it is not clear how far the genitive determiner in the example below implies the existence of a superset.
    (i) **Bill's** book is on the table.
    In this case, the genitive noun phrase *Bill's* does not imply that further referents of the type "book" are contextually available unless it receives contrastive stress. Example (i) can be uttered felicitously in a context where just one object of the type book is available. Its interpretation in that context could be roughly paraphrased as, "There is an object on the table which is a book that happens to belong to Bill." If there is contrastive stress on the genitive noun phrase an alternative is implied.
    (ii) **BILL's** book is on the table.

136 *Notes*

The utterance in example (ii) is only felicitous if there are more books that belong to someone other than Bill. Thus, this case suggests that the presence of (contrastive) focus is the crucial factor.

16. This is based on the "Contrast Condition on Nominal Ellipsis" presented by Giannakidou and Stavrou (1999), which is very similar to Eguren's.

A nominal subconstituent α can be elided in constituent β only if the remnant β of is not identical to the corresponding part of the antecedent γ of α (Giannakidou & Stavrou 1999: 305).

NOTES TO CHAPTER 4

1. The exact relation between *one* and its silent counterpart will be discussed in Section 4.3.
2. For a more concise version of this discussion, the reader is referred to Günther 2011.
3. Elsewhere, a further distinction is drawn between contrastive focus and information focus (see, e.g., É. Kiss's highly influential 1998 paper). However, the boundaries between the two are blurred: An example such as (i) is considered contrastive by Kenesei (2006), because a complementary subset (the authors who may have written the novel) is active. According to É. Kiss this is noncontrastive, because the alternatives are not identified.
   (i) Who wrote War and Peace?
       It was Tolstoy who wrote *War and Peace.*
       (É. Kiss 1998: 268; also in Kenesei 2006: 141)
   The lack of clarity reflected here leads some authors to assume that contrastiveness is a gradient phenomenon. Bolinger, for example, states that "in a broad sense every semantic peak is contrastive" (1961: 87; see Lambrecht 1994 for a similar conception of contrastiveness). What all these different understandings of contrast have in common is that alternatives and sets play a role. The major differences to be found in the approaches outlined above result from differing restrictions imposed on the set of alternatives. This set can either be open or closed; if it is a closed set, that is, when there is a limited number of alternatives to be excluded, the set members can either be contextually given or explicitly mentioned. Hence, although there is considerable disagreement on what contrast is, it is generally acknowledged that contrast is an operation on alternatives, whatever exact configuration the latter set may have.
4. Dahl (1985: 68) presents another example to point out that both noun phrases can be coreferential.
   (i) I'd like to marry an intelligent man and a reliable one.
   This example allows for both the bigamous and monogamous reading.However, these noun phrases are attributive rather than referential in the sense of Donnellan (1966). I doubt that they could be interpreted as referring to one particular individual.
5. To simplify this description, I only consider referential cases at this point.
6. According to Bouchard, number is semantically coded only once in a noun phrase. In English, this is on the head noun and in French it is on the determiner, as Bouchard demonstrates by a series of tests. In English, prenominal elements such as numerals or demonstratives express number through agreement but not semantically. This is why, according to Bouchard, the noun cannot be left out as easily as in French. As a detailed discussion of this account is certainly beyond the scope of the present work, suffice it to point out one

Notes 137

problematic aspect. Noun ellipsis in German, as illustrated in Chapter 2, is much freer than in English. However, Bouchard assumes that number is on N here as well. The flexibility in terms of ellipsis is attributed to adjectival inflection—"adjectives may bear one of the nominal features" (ibid.: 234). It is not clear why agreement allows for ellipsis here but it does not in English (structures such as *those green* should be licit under such an approach).

7. In Chapter 2 it was pointed out that under certain circumstances adjectives are licit without *one*. The discussion of this phenomenon is postponed to Chapter 5.

8. They can, of course, also be followed by a lexical noun.

9. Recall that discourse-referential elements are considered contrastive because of this alternative-indicating property (see Eguren 2010).

10. Allan (1980) assumes that countability is a property of the entire nominal phrase rather than the noun. Whether countability is determined lexically or structurally is not relevant at this point, and the discussion will be taken up in Section 4.3.2.

11. For a classification of elements according to which anaphoric element they take—a silent noun, stressed or unstressed *one*, see Dahl 1985: 26–28.

12. As an anonymous reviewer points out, this is incompatible with Link's analyses of the definite article as bringing about individuation and countability in its semantics (Link 1983). However, even though a definite expression refers to a particular instance of a mass and hence has a portioning function, this does not make the noun phrase structurally countable. Evidence for this derives from a ban on *one*-insertion with mass antecedents, as mentioned in Section 4.2:
    (i) *The advice you gave was more useful than the one I received from the Dean. (= example 23a)
    I follow Borer's (2005) claim that the definite article serves as a discourse anaphor that copies the mass count-properties of the antecedent onto the structure. I come back to the structural view of countability in Section 4.3.2.2.

13. the one (_PUN| _VBB| _VBZ| _VDD| _VDZ| _VHD| _VHZ| _VM0| _VVB| _VVD| _VVZ) and the ones (_PUN| _VBB| _VBZ| _VDD| _VDZ| _VHD| _VHZ| _VM0| _VVB| _VVD| _VVZ). Some instances had to be excluded as they were not tagged properly, such as in (i):
    (i) ... that budget was better than **the one put forward by the Labour**. (BNC, KRL 2341)

14. For a detailed overview of ellipsis accounts in general the reader is referred to Klein 1993, Winkler 2006, Merchant 2012, and Reich 2011.

15. I am fully aware of the criticisms that have been raised against such a rather traditional approach to word classes and their definitions (for an overview, see Aarts 2004a, 2004b, and for a detailed critical analysis, see Croft 2001, 2007). However, I assume that in this case an approach that takes word classes to be discrete entities is fully justified. One could argue, of course, that the remnant element is neither a noun nor an adjective, and assign it to a category in between the two, or to allow for the two categories to overlap. Categories such as word classes may be gradient in some cases but here an account arguing for fuzzy boundaries would overlook the regularity behind this phenomenon. It will be demonstrated that the structure of noun ellipsis constructions directly results from the general architecture of the nominal domain and that a systemic linguistic approach can capture the empirical facts without resorting to gradience.

16. Please note that PF-deletion is relevant for the current proposal, because I assume that *one* can be phonologically deleted (similar to what is proposed by Ross 1969). For a detailed discussion, see Section 4.3.1.

138   *Notes*

17. In Barbier's account NumP is the highest projection, i.e., it dominates DP.
18. Compare also Kayne's (2003) analysis of *the others* as the *other ONEs*.
19. Note that numeral *one* requires deletion of nominal *one*. However, in this case the haplology effect is more than obvious.
20. Note that, contrary to the claim by Stirling and Huddleston (2002), some speakers seem to find *these ones* and *those ones* acceptable. The BNC renders 87 hits for *these ones* and 57 for *those ones*. Cardinal numerals, on the other hand, are not followed by an adjacent *one*. The only hits in the BNC are those where the element does not function as a numeral but as a nonanaphoric lexical noun (*ones* as opposed to *tens*, for example, as dollar bills, etc.):
    (i) These are ones here, you see that's saying we've got four tens, forty, and then we've got **nine ones,** so that's how we get forty-nine. (BNC, JJS 69)
    These examples clearly have to be kept apart from the phenomenon of *one-*insertion. However, a larger corpus such as the COCA, provides examples of numerals used with *ones* (taken from Günther 2012, note16).
    (ii) He was building one radio of **two ones,** so we also were able to listen long wave. (COCA, 2008 ACAD)
    (iii) Here, of course, most of those seats are gerrymandered but here are **four ones** that could be something. (COCA, 2003 SPOK)
    (iv) A careful look at Table VI revealed that the preferred leisure activities indicated by the undergraduates showed that out of the eleven activities preferred by the undergraduates, **the first seven ones** are indoor games. (COCA, 2007 ACAD)
    (v) . . . a report on the number of slaves imported within 89 years to the Spanish colonies. There were **473,000 ones** brought and only 224,000 remained (COCA, 2008 ACAD)
    (vi) Well, if you look at the home furnishings industry, and we are most probably one of the **few ones** that is doing as well. (COCA, 2001 SPOK)
    These examples illustrates that the rule formulated in example (91) can be relaxed for some speakers, that is, there is considerable variation, which provides further support for the hypothesis that the choice between silent noun and one is not determined by syntax.
21. The need for number disambiguation is considered as evidence for a licensing mechanism that applies to functional but not to lexical categories by Llombart-Huesca (2002). An empty number head for example needs to be licensed because functional properties cannot be recovered from elsewhere. The lexical noun, in contrast, can be recovered because of its antecedent, therefore, it does not need licensing and can be elided freely, according to Llombart-Huesca (2002).
22. The choice between *one* and a silent noun in those cases where it is clearly optional is governed by pragmatic factors to be discussed in Chapter 5.
23. Günther (2012) points out that *stuff* can be used as anaphoric mass noun, as in the example below, which shows an instance of *stuff* referring back to *food.*
    (i) . . . the right food can enhance performance and **the wrong stuff** can cripple mountaineers. (COCA, 1997 NEWS)
24. Note that Cheng and Sybesma (1999) argue that these two types of classification reflect a mass-count distinction that is inherent to nouns. The so-called massifiers are required to create countable units when they are used with mass nouns (they can be used with count nouns as well—*three groups of people*). The nouns in example (97), however, "provide natural units by which they can be counted" (ibid.: 515). Therefore, Cheng and Sybesma claim that the classifiers used here do not produce countable units, they only name them.

Notes 139

Borer (2005) in contrast argues that the mass-count distinction is not lexically but structurally encoded. Consider the following counterexample from Borer (2005: 98), which displays an (ontological) count noun, *shu* "book" used with a "massifier."

(i) liang xiang (de) shu
two CL-box de book

For a more detailed discussion the reader is referred to ibid.: 97–101.

25. Borer (2005: 95) provides further support for this claim. In Armenian, where both strategies are available, numeral classifiers and plural morphology on the head noun are in complementary distribution.

(i) a. Yergu had hovanoc uni-m.
two CL umbrella have-1SG

"I have two umbrellas."

b. Yergu hovanoc-ner unim.
two umbrella-PL have-1SG

"I have two umbrellas."

c. *Yergu had havanoc-ner unim.
two CL umbrella-PL have-1SG

"I have two umbrellas."

26. The following example from Borer 2005: 102 illustrates that the same noun can be used in both contexts:

(i) a. a wine, a love, a thread, a salt, a stone
b. wines, loves, threads, salts, stones
c. We store three bloods in this lab.
d. there is dog/stone/chicken on this floor
e. that's quite a bit of table/carpet for the money
f. (too) much dog/chicken, (too) much stone, (too) much table

27. For the sake of completeness, it should be pointed out that there are attested uses of a possessive determiner:

(i) In some cases, What's being done, for **our disabled?** (BNC, BM4 1122)
(ii) to help families who did not have enough money to bury their dead. (BNC, ABU 1390)

Other types of determiners can be used as well:

(iii) "**These dead** are my responsibility," replied the policeman. (BNC, H84 2287)
(iv) In addition to those unemployed who are not claiming benefits . . . (BNC, BNW 280)

However, Quirk et al. state that "[t]he definite determiner is normally the generic definite article *the*" (1985: 423). For a detailed analysis of the human and the Abstract Construction in English and German, the reader is referred to Günther (in preparation).

28. Payne and Huddleston (2002: 417) mention *the accused, the deceased* as cases that are not necessarily used generically. Singular reference is possible as well.

29. They present the below examples (Cheng & Sybesma 1999: 511).

(i) Zek gau zungji sek juk. Cantonese
CL dog like eat meat

"The dog likes to eat meat." not "Dogs like to eat meat."

(ii) Ngo zungji tong zek gau waan.
I like with CL dog play

"I like to play with the dog." not "'I like to play with dogs."

See also Senft (2000) and references therein. Senft claims that "a classifier marks that the noun it classifies must be understood as having non-generic

140 *Notes*

reference, in other words: classifiers individuate nouns in classifier languages" (2000: 27).

30. Alexiadou et al. claim that "definite plurals are never used for genericity, regardless of the precise interpretation" (2007: 177). Lyons (1991, 1999), however, states that certain nouns denoting classes of classes such as *dinosaur* or *vertebrate* can be used in definite plural noun phrases and still receive a generic reading.
    (i) The dinosaurs were the biggest creatures on earth.
    (ii) The vertebrates have a great advantage in the evolutionary race. (Lyons 1991: 114)

31. According to Quirk et al. *people* can be added while retaining genericity. However, they note that in those cases, "the definite determiner is normally omitted" (1985: 422).

32. This might suggests that *one* is a kind of classifier as claimed by Llombart-Huesca 2002 and Alexiadou and Gengel, Chapter 3. However, I consider *one* as a noun that hosts a classifierlike element, i.e., number.

33. This is just the morphosyntactic condition on noun ellipsis—as in English, the felicitous use of elliptical noun phrases is subject to the contrast condition.

34. It should be emphasized that this holds if the elements constitute the only item in the noun phrase—when they are followed by adjectives, they remain uninflected. Adjacency plays a role for noun ellipsis in German as well, as will be outlined in the course of this section.

35. Lobeck (1995: 134) lists the following strong agreement features for German.
    a. definite and indefinite determiners: plural: [+Case, +Plural], singular: [+Case, +Gender], other: [+Poss]
    b. quantifiers: plural: [+ Case, +Plural, +Partitive], singular: [+ Case, +Gender, +Partitive]
    c. numerals: plural: [+Plural, +Partitive], singular: [+ Case, +Gender, +Partitive]
    d. adjectives: plural: [+Case, +Plural], singular: [+Case, +Gender]

36. Remember that Lobeck (1995) assumes that three features license noun ellipsis in English: partitivity, plural, and possessive.

37. A counterexample to gender as the crucial property comes from the elliptical use of cardinal numerals. First, they can remain uninflected. Second, the endings that occur only in elliptical contexts in Present Day German encode case rather than gender.

NOTES TO CHAPTER 5

1. The term *adjective* as used in this chapter refers to descriptive adjectives and excludes the discourse-referential ones such as *next, same,* and *other,* which do not attribute properties. When reference is made to the differences between the two types of adjectives, distinct labels will be used.

2. A more concise version of the corpus study can be found in Günther 2011, but some aspects are not addressed, such as accessibility theory and its applicability to anaphora below noun phrase level.

3. Note that *following* is problematic in that it often has a meaning similar to that of the Abstract Construction, which can be paraphrased roughly as "that what follows." This is displayed in (i). In (ii) it is not clear whether *the following* contains an silent noun with *example* as the antecedent—inserting *example* would yield an acceptable structure—or whether it has the meaning of "that what follows" as well.

(i) **The following** is a summary of the principal conditions of the Loan Protector policy and is provided for general information purposes only. (BNC, AYP 2353)

(ii) Compare the previous example with **the following**. (BNC, A0M 1075)

4. I owe thanks to David Denison for a useful comment on this matter.

5. The question that may arise here is why it is the first one thousand adjectives that were taken. There are several reasons. As will be pointed out in Section 5.2, there is a correlation between the adjectives that featured most frequently in noun ellipsis contexts and their position in the frequency list for the whole BNC. Given that noun ellipsis with adjectival modifiers is a rare phenomenon in English, one can expect that less frequent adjectives do not appear in the ellipsis construction.

   Apart from the fact that one would probably not find a significant number of hits that match the relevant requirements, it would take too much time to search for them and then manually extract them—there are 98,276 different items tagged as AJ0 in the BNC. It should be noted that a quantitative analysis of a marginal phenomenon is hardly fruitful; thus, the focus in this work is on qualitative data. Moreover, as the focus in this chapter is on contextual aspects, an all-inclusive list of adjectives that occur in noun ellipsis constructions is not required here.

6. There are 54 hits for *red*, 34 for *blue*, 12 for *black*, 10 for *yellow*, 6 for *white*, 5 for *green*, 4 for *pink*, and 2 hits for *grey*. Furthermore, *lemon* and *brown* show up once.

7. *Black* occurs 17 times, *red* 14 times, *white* and *blue* 13 times each. There are 11 hits for *yellow*, 9 for *grey*, 6 for *green*, 3 for *pink*, and 3 for *brown*. *Silvergrey, lemon, red pied, black pied, white and red, gold,* and *golden* appear once.

8. Probably the speakers are playing The Very Hungry Caterpillar Game, a game that involves 40 "food pieces," small cardboard pieces that come in different colors (http://www.ugames.com/rules/university_games/TheVeryHungryCaterpillarGame.html).

9. They do so in order to reduce complexity—information that is accessible does not have to be computed again. An illustrative quote comes from Kehler (2000).

   But forms such as ellipsis appear to *reduce* the computational burden on the hearer rather than increase it; apparently, avoiding the need to recompute existing and readily recoverable information offsets the cost of accessing the referent. (546)

10. In three instances of the Taxonimizing Construction the elliptical noun phrases are indefinite—the indefinite article is used twice (i), and in one case the elliptical noun phrases contain the indefinite numeral *one* (ii).

    (i) Then came two bays, **a light** and **a dark**. (BNC, H8B 2083)

    (ii) There is a choice of two covers, **a white** and **a gold,** to make the displays stand out. (BNC, GWL 931)

    (iii) devout Jews were anxiously awaiting the advent of two Messiahs—**one royal from David, one priestly from Aaron**— . . . (BNC, EDY 1576)

11. This, of course, is reminiscent of the notion of construction in Construction Grammar as a stored form-meaning pairing (see, e.g., Goldberg 1995). I will not pursue the applicability of this particular framework any further in the present work.

12. Note that this understanding of partitivity differs from Sleeman's general notion of partitivity, defined as "properly or improperly included within" (1996: 34). Recall from Chapter 3 that there are, for example, cardinal numerals and universal quantifiers among the elements with an inherent partitive meaning

142 *Notes*

(D-partitives). These are not partitive in the sense of Bouchard (2002), that is, a use of a cardinal numeral does not presuppose the existence of a further referent such as the discourse-referential modifiers (*next, other, same, first, second,* and so forth) do. Sleeman's concept of partitivity presented in terms of classifying adjectives, however, resembles Bouchard's. Once again, this implies that the notion of partitivity is rather vague and does not refer to a uniform phenomenon (for detailed criticism of this concept the reader is referred to Chapter 3).

13. Further findings within the lexical realm were the use of expressions that encode differences between referents, such as the adjective *different* and the verbal construction *to tell from.*
    (i) ... if the new use is "substantially" *different from* **the old** (BNC, B2D 684) (= example 55)
    (ii) Pascoe could *tell* a good lie *from* **a bad.** (BNC, FP7 2011) (= example 58)
    However, this also the effect of, rather than the cause for, noun ellipsis—if different instances of the same kind are made reference to within one proposition, it is hardly surprising that lexical expressions encoding similarities and differences are to be found within these contexts.

14. This also holds for what can be used as a classifying adjective. What results in natural classification is rather difficult to define as already pointed out by Bolinger (1967), who discusses the properties of attributive modification in English. Although there is compounding of the type *the home-loving girl* and *your letter-writing friends,* this is not fully productive but constrained by pragmatic factors—there are neither **mistake-erasing secretaries* nor **husband-waking wives.* Attributive elements must result in a plausible characterization. The unacceptable examples "must wait the day when we have some interest in characterizing secretaries as mistake-erasing or wives as husband-waking" (ibid.: 6f).

15. Another interesting aspect is that the adjectives that always imply the paradigmatic contrast as described above rarely occur on their own. Of the remaining 280 instances of adjectives that are not used with a modifier of the same type only very few are of this "inherently contrastive" nature. *Good* occurs twice, *long* four times, *old* four times as well, *young* only once and *new* appears twice without *old* (or *aged*) within the context. This also underlines that it is the context rather than a particular adjectival class that allows for the use of silent nouns.

16. (_AT0| _AVQ| _CJS| _CJT| _DPS| _DTQ| _EX0| _ITJ| _PNP| _PNQ| _PNX| _POS| _PRF| _PRP| .| !| \?| ;| _PUR| _TO0| _VBB| _VBD| _VBG| _VBI| _VBN| _VDB| _VDD| _VDG| _VBZ| _VDI| _VDN| _VDZ| _VHD| _VHB| _VHG| _VHI| _VHN| _VHZ| _VM0| _VVB| _VVD| _VVG| _VVI| _VVZ| _XX0) (= example 1c), for an explanation cf. Section 5.1.

17. There was one example that might be considered to fulfill the criteria:
    (i) The early trees, like their predecessors, the mosses, existed in two alternating forms, *a sexual generation* and *an asexual one.* (EFR 899)
    However, this was excluded because the antecedent, *form,* is not identical to the lexical noun in the first conjunct, *generation.*

18. There are 26 hits for *spoken discourse* and 27 for *written discourse.*

19. It is worthwhile mentioning that the term "kind" is adopted in a rather loosely defined sense in this section. Strictly speaking, we are not dealing with kinds and subkinds here but with concepts and subconcepts. In contrast to concepts, kinds are well-established. Krifka (1995) describes the difference as follows:
    Similar to kinds, concepts are abstract entities related to real objects. However, they need not be well-established, but could be construed from scratch.

Furthermore, concepts may stand in a subconcept relation (as, e.g., a gentleman wearing blue clothes is a gentleman), but not necessarily in a taxonomic relation (it is not a subspecies of gentleman). (Krifka 1995: 402).

However, as Krifka et al. (1995:11n9) remark, they do not set out to clarify what exactly counts as well-established kind.

20. This does not hold for every instance of noun ellipsis and *one*-insertion because non-identity can also obtain on the linguistic level (see Section 4.1). A restricted range of adjectives (e.g., *same* or *very*) allows the anaphoric phrase to be coreferential with the antecedent phrase. Still, the modifier expresses hearer-new information because if a speaker does not substitute a pronoun for the full noun phrase, he or she does so in order to add something to the description. In other words, if the answer is *No, I think I'd like to keep the same ones* instead of *No, I think I'd like to keep them,* the fact that the speaker wants to keep exactly those pictures is emphasized and, thus, new to the hearer.

21. In most cases, one of the modifiers is used with the antecedent, the other with an silent noun. However, one instance of the Taxonomizing Construction occurred:

(i) The Act provides for two procedures for extradition between the United Kingdom and foreign states, **the new** and **the old.** (BNC, FDJ 100)

22. A Kruskal-Wallis-Test (Chi-square 30,378, df 2, asymptotic significance ,000) indicated the need for nonparametric tests. The relations between the distances for (a) silent and lexical noun, (b) silent noun and *one*, and (c) lexical noun and *one* were thus analyzed with Mann-Whitney Tests.

Anaphor-antecedent distances

	a	b	c
Mann-Whitney-U	203,000	751,500	1892,000
Wilcoxon-W	581,000	1129,500	10277,000
Z	−4,457	−4,705	−2,7775
Asymptotic significance (2 sided)	,000	,000	,006
Exact significance (2 sided)	,000	,000	,005
Exact significance (1 sided)	,000	,000	,003
Point probability	,000	,000	,000

References

CORPORA

BNC: *British National Corpus*
COCA: *Corpus of Contemporary American English*
Deutsches Referenzkorpus

B97: *Berliner Zeitung*, 1997
B98: *Berliner Zeitung*, 1998
B03: *Berliner Zeitung*, 2003
B05: *Berliner Zeitung*, 2005
B07: *Berliner Zeitung*, 2007
BRZ08: *Braunschweiger Zeitung*, 2008
BRZ09: *Braunschweiger Zeitung*, 2009
DPA09: *Deutsche Presse-Agentur*, 2009
HAZ07: *Hannoversche Allgemeine*, 2007
HAZ08: *Hannoversche Allgemeine*, 2008
HMP09: *Hamburger Morgenpost*, 2009
M07: *Mannheimer Morgen*, 2007
NUN09: *Nürnberger Nachrichten*, 2009
RHZ06: *Rhein-Zeitung*, 2006
RHZ07: *Rhein-Zeitung*, 2007
RHZ09: *Rhein-Zeitung*, 2009
SOZ08: *Die Südostschweiz*, 2008
THM: *Thomas-Mann-Korpus*
Z07: *Die Zeit*, 2007

SECONDARY SOURCES

Aarts, Bas. 2004a. "Conceptions of Gradience in the History of Linguistics." *Language Sciences* 26:343–389.

Aarts, Bas. 2004b. "Modelling Linguistic Gradience." *Studies in Language* 28(1):1–49.

Abney, Steven. 1987. "The English Noun Phrase in its Sentential Aspect." PhD diss., MIT, Cambridge, MA.

Aboh, Enoch O. 2004. "Topic and Focus within D." *Linguistics in the Netherlands* 21:1–12.

Alexiadou, Artemis, and Kirsten Gengel. Forthcoming. "NP Ellipsis Without Focus Movement/Projections: The Role of Classifiers." To appear in *Contrasts and Positions in Information Structure,* edited by Ivona Kučerová and Ad Neeleman. Cambridge: Cambridge University Press.

146   *References*

Alexiadou, Artemis, Liliane Haegeman, and Melita Stavrou. 2007. *Noun Phrase in the Generative Perspective.* Berlin: Mouton de Gruyter.

Allan, Keith. 1977. "Classifiers." *Language* 53:285–311.

Allan, Keith. 1980. "Nouns and Countability." *Language* 56:541–74.

Ariel, Mira. 1990. *Accessing Noun Phrase Antecedents.* London: Routledge.

Ariel, Mira. 2001. "Accessibility Theory: An Overview." In *Text Representation,* edited by Ted Sanders, Joost Schliperoord, and Wilbert Spooren, 29–87. Amsterdam: John Benjamins.

Barbiers, Sjef. 2005. "Variation in the Morphosyntax of 'One.'" *Journal of Comparative Germanic Linguistics* 8(3):159–83.

Bauer, Laurie. 1983. *English Word-Formation.* Cambridge: Cambridge University Press.

Beghelli, Filippo, and Tim Stowell. 1997. "Distributivity and Negation: The Syntax of *Each* and *Every.*" In *Ways of Scope Taking,* edited by Anna Szabolcsi, 71–107. Dordrecht: Kluwer.

Bolinger, Dwight. 1961. "Contrastive Accent and Contrastive Stress." *Language* 37:83–96.

Bolinger, Dwight. 1967. "Adjectives in English: Attribution and Predication." *Lingua* 18:1–34.

Borer, Hagit. 2005. *In Name Only: Structuring Sense.* Vol. 1, New York: Oxford University Press.

Borer, Hagit, and Isabelle Roy. 2010. "The Name of the Adjective." In *Adjectives: Formal Analyses in Syntax and Semantics,* edited by Patricia Cabredo Hofherr and Ora Matushansky, 85–114. Amsterdam: John Benjamins.

Bouchard, Denis. 2002. *Adjectives, Number and Interfaces–Why Languages Vary.* Amsterdam: Elsevier.

Cheng, Lisa, and Rint Sybesma. 1999. "Bare and Not-So-Bare Nouns and the Structure of NP." *Linguistic Inquiry* 30:509–42.

Conklin, Nancy F. 1981. "The Semantics and Syntax in Numeral Classification in Tai and Austronesian." PhD thesis, University of Michigan.

Corbett, Greville. 1991. *Gender.* New York: Cambridge University Press.

Corver, Norbert, and Marjo van Koppen. 2009. "Let's Focus on Noun Phrase Ellipsis." *Groninger Arbeiten zur Germanistischen Linguistik* 48:3–26.

Corver, Norbert, and Marjo van Koppen. 2011. "NP-Ellipsis with Adjectival Remnants: A Micro-comparative Perspective." *Natural Language and Linguistic Theory* 29:371–421.

Croft, William. 1994. "Semantic Universals in Classifier Systems." *Word* 45:145–71.

Croft, William. 2001. *Radical Construction Grammar: Syntactic Theory in Typological Perspective.* New York: Oxford University Press.

Croft, William. 2007. "Beyond Aristotle and Gradience: A Reply to Aarts." *Studies in Language* 31(2):409–30.

Dahl, Deborah. 1985. *The Structure and Function of* One-*Anaphora in English.* Bloomington: Indiana University Linguistics Club.

de Belder, Marijke. 2011. "A Morphosyntactic Decomposition of Countability in Germanic." *Journal of Comparative Germanic Linguistics* 14(3):173–202.

Dixon, R. M. W. 1977. "Where Have All the Adjectives Gone?" *Studies in Language* 1:19–80.

Dixon, R. M. W. 1982. *Where Have All the Adjectives Gone? and Other Essays in Semantics and Syntax.* Berlin: Mouton.

Donnellan, Keith S. 1966. "Reference and Definite Descriptions." *The Philosophical Review* 75(3):281–304.

Downing, Pamela. 1986. "The Anaphoric Use of Classifiers in Japanese." In *Noun Classes and Categorization: Proceedings of a Symposium on Categorization and Noun Classification, Eugene, Oregon, October 1983,* edited by Colette Craig, 345–75. Amsterdam: John Benjamins.

References   147

Duden. 2009. *Die Grammatik*. 8th rev. ed. Mannheim: Dudenverlag.

Eguren, Luis. 2010. "Contrastive Focus and Nominal Ellipsis in Spanish." *Lingua* 120(22):435–57.

Eisenberg, Peter. 2006. *Das Wort: Grundriss der deutschen Grammatik*. Vol. 1, 3rd ed. Stuttgart: Metzler.

É. Kiss, Katalin. 1998. "Identificational Focus Versus Information Focus." *Language* 74(2):245–273.

Embick, David, and Rolf Noyer. 2001. "Movement Operations After Syntax." *Linguistic Inquiry* 32:555–95.

Enç, Mürvet. 1991. "The Semantics of Specificity." *Linguistic Inquiry* 22:1–25.

Fillmore, Charles. 1976. "Pragmatics and the Description of Discourse." In *Pragmatik/Pragmatics 2*, edited by Siegfried Schmidt, 83–104. Munich: Fink.

Fillmore, Charles. 1982. "Frame Semantics." In *Linguistics in the Morning Calm*, edited by Paul Kiparsky, 111–137. Seoul: Hanshin.

Fitzpatrick, Justin Michael. 2006. "The Syntactic and Semantic Roots of Floating Quantification." PhD diss., MIT, Cambridge, MA.

Gengel, Kirsten. 2007. "Focus and Ellipsis. " PhD diss., Stuttgart.

Giannakidou, Anastasia, and Melita Stavrou. 1999. "Nominalization and Ellipsis in the Greek DP." *Linguistic Review* 16(44):295–331.

Goldberg, Adele E. 1995. *Constructions: A Construction Grammar Approach to Argument Structure*. Chicago: University of Chicago Press.

González-Alvarez, Dolores, Ana Elina Martínez-Insua, Javier Pérez-Guerra, and Esperanza Rama-Martínez, eds. 2011. Special issue on the structure of the noun phrase in English: Synchronic and diachronic explorations. *English Language and Linguistics* 15(2).

Greenberg, Joseph. 1978. "How Does a Language Acquire Gender-markers?" In *Universals of Human Language*, vol. 3: *Word Structure*, edited by Joseph Greenberg, 47–82. Stanford, CA: Stanford University Press.

Grinevald, Colette. 2000. "A Morphosyntactic Typology of Classifiers." In *Systems of Nominal Classification*, edited by Gunther Senft, 50–92. Cambridge: Cambridge University Press.

Günther, Christine. 2011. "Noun Ellipsis in English: Adjectival Modifiers and the Role of Context." *English Language & Linguistics* 15(2):279–301.

Günther, Christine. 2012. "Restating the Obvious—Some (Not So New) Thoughts on '-'Substantivized' Adjectives." Manuscript, Institut für Deutsche Sprache.

Günther, Christine. In preparation. "Substantivisch gebrauchte Adjektive." Manuscript, Institut für Deutsche Sprache.

Halliday, Michael A. K. 1985. *An Introduction to Functional Grammar*. London: Arnold.

Halliday, Michael, and Ruqiaya Hasan. 1976. *Cohesion in English*. London: Longman.

Heck, Fabian, Gereon Müller, and Jochen Trommer. 2008. "A Phase-Based Approach to Scandinavian Definiteness Marking." In *Proceedings of the 26th West Coast Conference on Formal Linguistics*, edited by Charles Chang and Hannah Haynie, 226–33. Sommerville, MA: Cascadilla Proceedings Project.

Hoffmann, Sebastian, Stefan Evert, Nicholas Smith, David Lee, and Ylva Berglund Prytz. 2008. *Corpus Linguistics with BNCweb:A Practical Guide. English Corpus Linguistics*. Vol. 6, Frankfurt am Main: Peter Lang.

van Hoof, Hanneke. 2005. "What Stranded Adjectives Reveal about Split-NP Topicalization." In *Organizing Grammar: Studies in Honor of Henk van Riemsdijk*, edited by Hans Broekhuis, Norbert Corver, Riny Huybregts, Ursula Kleinhenz, and Jan Koster, 230–40. Berlin: Mouton de Gruyter.

Huddleston, Rodney, and Geoffrey K. Pullum. 2002. *The Cambridge Grammar of the English Language*. Cambridge: Cambridge University Press.

Jackendoff, Ray. 1977. *X-bar Syntax: A Study of Phrase Structure*. Cambridge, MA: MIT Press.

148   *References*

Jespersen, Otto. 1933. *Essentials of English Grammar.* London: Routledge.
Johnson, Kyle. 2001. "What VP Ellipsis Can Do, and What It Can't, but Not Why." In *The Handbook of Contemporary Syntactic Theory,* edited by Mark Baltin and Chris Collins, 439–79. Malden, MA: Blackwell.
Jones, Michael Allan. 1993. *Sardinian Syntax.* London: Routledge.
Kayne, Richard. 2003. "Silent Years, Silent Hours." In *Grammar in Focus: Festschrift for Christer Platzack,* edited by Lars-Olof Delsing, Gunlög Josefsson, Halldór Sigurdsson, and Cecilia Falk, 209–26. Lund: Wallin and Dalholm.
Kehler, Andrew. 2000. "Coherence and the Resolution of Ellipsis." *Linguistics and Philosophy* 23(6):533–75
Keizer, Evelien. 2007. The English Noun Phrase: The Nature of Linguistic Categorization. Cambridge: Cambridge University Press.
Keizer, Evelien. 2011. "English Proforms: An Alternative Account." *English Language & Linguistics* 15(2):303–34.
Kenesei, István. 2006. "Focus as Identification." In *The Architecture of Focus,* edited by Valéria Molnár and Susanne Winkler, 137–68. Berlin: Mouton de Gruyter.
Kester, Ellen-Petra. 1996a. "Adjectival Inflection and the Licensing of Empty Categories in DP." *Journal of Linguistics* 32:57–78.
Kester, Ellen-Petra. 1996b. "The Nature of Adjectival Inflection." PhD diss., Utrecht University.
Klein, Wolfgang. 1993. "Ellipse." In *Syntax: Ein internationales Handbuch zeitgenössischer Forschung,* edited by Joachim Jacobs, Theo Vennemann, Wolfgang Sternefeld, and Arnim von Stechow, 763–99. Vol. 1, Berlin: Mouton de Gruyter.
Krifka, Manfred. 1995. "Common Nouns: A Contrastive Analysis of English and Chinese." In *The Generic Book,* edited by Gregory N. Carlson and Francis Jeffry Pelletier, 398–411.Chicago: University of Chicago Press.
Krifka, Manfred. 2007. "Basic Notions of Information Structure." In *Interdisciplinary Studies on Information Structure. Working papers of the SFB 632,* edited by Carolin Féry, Gisbert Fanselow, and Manfred Krifka, 13–55. Vol. 6, Potsdam: Universitätsverlag.
Krifka, Manfred, Francis J. Pelletier, Gregory N. Carlson, Alice ter Meulen, Gennaro Chierchia, and Godehard Link. 1995. "Introduction to Genericity." In *The Generic Book,* edited by Gregory N. Carlson and Francis Jeffry Pelletier, 1–124. Chicago: University of Chicago Press.
Lambrecht, Knud. 1994. Information Structure and Sentence Form: Topic, Focus, and the Mental Representation of Discourse Referents. Cambridge: Cambridge University Press.
Link, Godehard. 1983. "The Logical Analysis of Plurals and Mass Terms: A Lattice Theoretical Approach." In *Meaning, Use, and the Interpretation of Language,* edited by Rainer Bäuerle, Christoph Schwarze, and Arnim von Stechow, 302–23. Berlin: Walter de Gruyter.
Llombart-Huesca, Amalia. 2002. "Anaphoric *One* and NP-Ellipsis." *Studia Linguistica* 56(1):59–89.
Lobeck, Anne. 1995. *Ellipsis: Functional Heads, Licensing, and Identification.* New York: Oxford University Press.
Lobeck, Anne. 2006. "Ellipsis in DP." In *The Blackwell Companion to Syntax,* edited by Martin Everaert and Henk van Riemsdijk, 145–73. Vol. 2, Malden, MA: Blackwell.
López, Luis. 2000. "Ellipsis and Discourse-Linking." *Lingua* 110:183–213.
Lyons, Christopher. 1991. "English Nationality Terms: Evidence for Dual Category Membership." *Journal of Literary Semantics* 20:97–116.
Lyons, Christopher. 1999. *Definiteness.* Cambridge: Cambridge University Press.
Merchant, Jason. 2001. *The Syntax of Silence: Sluicing, Islands, and the Theory of Ellipsis.* Oxford Studies in Theoretical Linguistics. Vol. 1, Oxford: Oxford University Press.

References   149

Merchant, Jason. 2012. "Ellipsis." Submitted for *Handbook of Contemporary Syntax* edited by Artemis Alexiadou, Tibor Kiss, and Miriam Butt. 2nd ed. Berlin: Walter de Gruyter.

Molnár, Valéria. 2006. "On Different Kinds of Contrast." In *Architecture of Focus,* edited by Valéria Molnár and Susanne Winkler, 197–233. *Studies in Generative Grammar.* Vol. 82, Berlin: Mouton de Gruyter.

Molnár, Valéria, and Susanne Winkler. 2010. "Edges and Gaps: Contrast at the Interfaces." *Lingua* 120:1392–1415.

Neeleman, Ad, and Hans van de Koot. 2006. "Syntactic Haplology." In The *Blackwell Companion to Syntax,* edited by Martin Everaert and Henk van Riemsdijk, 685–710. Vol. 4, Malden, MA: Blackwell.

Ngyuen, Dinh Hoa. 1957. "Classifiers in Vietnamese." *Word* 13:124–52.

Ntelitheos, Dimitris. 2004. "The Syntax of Elliptical and Discontinuous Nominals." MA thesis, University of California, Los Angeles.

Olsen, Susan. 1987. "Zum 'substantivierten' Adjektiv im Deutschen: Deutsch als eine pro-Drop-Sprache." *Studium Linguistik* 21:1–35.

Olsen, Susan. 1988. "Das 'substantivierte' Adjektiv im Deutschen und Englischen: Attribuierung vs. Syntaktische 'Substantivierung'. *Folia Linguistica* 22:337–72.

Overdiep, Gerrit. 1940. *De volkstaal van Katwijk aan Zee.* Antwerp: Standaard-Boekhandel.

Panagiotidis, Phoevos. 2002. *Pronouns, Clitics, and Empty Nouns.* Amsterdam: John Benjamins.

Panagiotidis, Phoevos. 2003a. "Empty Nouns." *Natural Language & Linguistic Theory* 21(2):381–432.

Panagiotidis, Phoevos. 2003b. "*One,* Empty Nouns, and Theta Assignment." *Linguistic Inquiry* 34:281–92.

Payne, John, and Rodney Huddleston. 2002. "Nouns and Noun Phrases." In *The Cambridge Grammar of the English Language,* edited by Rodney Huddleston and Geoffrey Pullum, 323–523. Cambridge: Cambridge University Press.

Perlmutter, David M. 1970. "On the Article in English." In *Progress in Linguistics,* edited by Manfred Bierwisch and Karl Erich Heidolph, 233–48. The Hague: Mouton.

Pesetsky, David. 1987. "Wh-in-Situ: Movement and Unselective Binding." In *The Representation of (In)definiteness,* edited by Eric Reuland and Alice G. B. ter Meulen, 98–128. Cambridge, MA: MIT Press.

Plag, Ingo. 2003. *Word-Formation in English.* Cambridge: Cambridge University Press.

Quirk, Randolph, Sidney Greenbaum, Geoffrey Leech, and Jan Svartvik. 1982. *A Grammar of Contemporary English.* Harlow: Longman.

Quirk, Randolph, Sidney Greenbaum, Geoffrey Leech, and Jan Svartvik. 1985. A *Comprehensive Grammar of the English Language.* London: Longman.

Radford, Andrew. 1989. "Profiling Proforms." Manuscript, University of Essex.

Reich, Ingo. 2011. "Ellipsis." In *Semantics: An International Handbook of Natural Language Meaning,* edited by Claudia Maienborn, Klaus von Heusinger and Paul Portner, 1849–74. Berlin: Mouton de Gruyter.

Repp, Sophie. 2010. "Defining 'Contrast' as an Information Structural Notion in Grammar." *Lingua* 120:1333–45.

Richards, Norvin. 2010. *Uttering Trees.* Cambridge, MA: MIT Press

Rijkhoff, Jan. 2008. "Descriptive and Discourse-Referential Modifiers in a Layered Model of the Noun Phrase." *Linguistics* 46(4):789–829.

Ritter, Elizabeth. 1991. "Two Functional Categories in Noun Phrases: Evidence from Modern Hebrew. In *Perspectives on Phrase Structure,* edited by Susan Rothstein, 37–62. *Syntax and Semantics.* Vol. 25, New York: Academic Press.

Rizzi, Luigi. 1986. "Null Objects in Italian and the Theory of *Pro.*" *Linguistic Inquiry* 17:501–57.

150 References

Rizzi, Luigi. 1997. "The Fine Structure of the Left Periphery. In *Elements of Grammar,* edited by Liliane Haegeman, 281–337. *Kluwer International Handbooks of Linguistics.* Vol. 1, Dordrecht: Kluwer.

Rooth, Mats. 1992. "A Theory of Focus Interpretation." *Natural Language Semantics* 1:75–116.

Ross, John R. 1967. "Constraints on Variables in Syntax." PhD diss., MIT, Cambridge, MA.

Saito, Mamoru, Jonah Lin, and Keiko Murasugi. 2008. "'N'-Ellipsis and the Structure of Noun Phrases in Chinese and Japanese." *Journal of East Asian Linguistics* 17:247–71.

Sauerland, Uli, and Kazuko Yatsushiro. 2004. "A Silent Noun in Partitives." In *Proceedings of NELS 34,* edited by Keir Moulton and Matthew Wolf, 101–112. Amherst: GLSA.

Schütze, Carson. 2001. "Semantically Empty Lexical Heads as Last Resorts." In *Semi-lexical Categories,* edited by Norbert Corver and Henk van Riemsdijk, 127–87. Berlin: Mouton de Gruyter.

Scott, Gary-John. 2002. "Stacked Adjectival Modification and the Structure of Nominal Phrases." In *Functional Structure in DP and IP: The Cartography of Syntactic Structures,* edited by Guglielmo Cinque, 91–120. New York: Oxford University Press.

Senft, Gunter. 2000. "What Do We Really Know about Nominal Classification Systems?" In *Systems of Nominal Classification,* edited by Gunter Senft, 11–49. Cambridge: Cambridge University Press.

Sleeman, Petra. 1996. "Licensing Empty Nouns in French." Dissertation, University of Amsterdam.

Sleeman, Petra. 2003. "Subnominal empty categories as subordinate topics." In *From NP to DP,* edited by Martin Coene and Yves D'hulst, 119–37. Vol. 1, Amsterdam: John Benjamins.

Sproat, Richard, and Chilin Shih. 1991. "The Cross-Linguistic Distribution of Adjective Ordering Restrictions." In *Interdisciplinary Approaches to Language,* edited by Carol Georgopoulos and Roberta Ishihara, 565–93. Dordrecht: Kluwer.

Stirling, Lesley, and Rodney Huddleston. 2002. "Deixis and Anaphora." In *The Cambridge Grammar of the English Language,* edited by Rodney Huddleston and Geoffrey Pullum, 1449–1566. Cambridge: Cambridge University Press.

Svenonius, Peter. 1994. "The Structural Location of the Attributive Adjective." In *The Proceedings of the Twelfth West Coast Conference on Formal Linguistics,* edited by Erin Duncan, Donka Farkas, and Philip Spaelti, 439–54. Stanford, CA: CSLI Publications.

Svenonius, Peter. 2008. "The Position of Adjectives and Other Phrasal Modifiers in the Decomposition of DP." In *Adjectives and Adverbs: Syntax, Semantics, and Discourse,* edited by Louise McNally and Chris Kennedy, 16–42. Oxford: Oxford University Press.

Tognini-Bonelli, Elena. 2001. *Corpus Linguistics at Work: Studies in Corpus Linguistics.* Vol. 6, Amsterdam: John Benjamins.

Valois, Daniel, and Phaedra Royle. 2009. "Partitivity, Atomization, and Noun-Drop: A Longitudinal Study of French Child Language." *Language Acquisition* 16(2):82–105.

Winkler, Susanne. 2005. *Ellipsis and Focus in Generative Grammar.* Studies in Generative Grammar. Vol. 81, Berlin: Mouton de Gruyter.

Winkler, Susanne. 2006. "Ellipsis." Manuscript, Universität Tübingen.

Zifonun, Gisela, Ludger Hoffman, and Bruno Strecker. 1997. *Grammatik der deutschen Sprache.* Berlin: Walter de Gruyter.

Index

A

Abstract Construction 2, 30, 72, 76–8, 89, 90, 120, 129, 133, 139, 140
accessibility 3, 4, 86, 94, 111, 118–19, 124–8, 132, 140
adjacency (of licensor and ellipsis site) 25, 48, 69–72, 75, 78, 81, 83–4, 130, 140
adjective: classifying, 31, 103–5, 135, 142; color 8, 11–12, 16, 32, 35, 85, 91, 93–4, 98–9, 104–5, 131; discourse-referential 6, 9–11, 29, 37, 43, 56, 58, 89, 103, 137, 140, 142; intersective 31, 135; noninflecting 16, 81; property-denoting 6, 7, 9, 11–13, 29, 57, 59, 61, 66, 72, 85, 91, 103, 126, 130–1, 140
adjective ordering 40, 134
Afrikaans 82–3
agreement 26–31, 41, 45–6, 66, 76, 80, 136–7, 140
American English 3–4
anaphora 3, 8–9, 22–4, 36–7, 43–4, 47, 50–4, 60–1, 63–4, 66, 69, 73, 75, 81, 83, 97, 104, 107, 111–12, 115, 118–19, 123–5, 127, 129–33, 133, 137–8, 140, 143
antecedent (type of) 25, 114–16, 125
antonym, 32, 98–102
argument structure (of nouns) 25. *See also* theta-marking
article: definite 5, 10, 13, 14, 50, 63–6, 72, 76, 97, 98, 107, 116, 137, 139; indefinite 8, 11, 15, 26, 70, 79, 98, 106, 134, 141

B

British English 3, 4

C

case 12, 16–17, 19, 27–9, 41, 78–80
Chinese 44, 73–4
classifier 21, 44–5, 48, 72–8, 80–1, 83, 116, 131, 138–40
classifier phrase 5, 44–5, 69, 75
comparative 11
complement 22, 25, 26, 34, 42, 69, 87, 102–3, 115, 116
contrast 12, 23, 25, 38–44, 47, 48–50, 52, 54–5, 59–61, 63, 69, 83, 85, 101–5, 128, 130–2, 134–7, 140, 142
contrastive focus *see* focus
contrastiveness *see* contrast
conversion 2, 67–8
countability 25, 29, 47, 48, 57–9, 63, 66, 68, 71, 72, 75, 83, 85, 106, 115, 130, 137
count-mass distinction 73–6. *See also* countability

D

definiteness 11, 14
deletion *see* phonological deletion
determiner 3–6, 8–16, 20, 26–7, 30, 37, 54, 57, 64, 67, 69, 83, 86–90, 105, 122, 135–6, 139, 140
discourse context 20, 64, 93–4, 113, 126
discourse-linking 30, 43, 135
distance (between anaphor and antecedent) 24, 111–13, 124–8, 132, 134, 143
double definiteness 69–70
Dutch 27, 28, 41–2, 44, 70–83

F

focus 21, 38, 39–44, 46–7, 49, 53, 55, 60, 70, 134, 136
French 27, 30–3, 81, 95, 103, 116, 136

152 Index

functional categories 5, 26, 28, 29, 31, 44, 45, 71, 75, 83, 84, 115, 131, 135, 138

G
gender 7, 12, 15, 27, 44, 74, 78–81, 83–4, 131, 140
genitive 6, 9, 10, 12, 15, 17, 29, 57, 59, 135
German 2, 4, 7–8, 12–19, 27–8, 44, 48, 74, 76, 78–83, 84, 131, 134–5, 137, 139–40

H
haplology 70, 83, 138
Head Movement Constraint 66–7
Human Construction 2, 76–8, 81, 89, 90, 116, 120, 129, 129, 131

I
inflection 2, 4, 12–19, 21, 25–31, 33, 39, 41–2, 46–7, 59, 63, 78, 81–4, 118, 131, 134, 137, 140

J
Japanese 44, 73

K
kind 31, 35, 54, 58, 75, 97, 104, 116–17, 127, 131, 142–3

L
linguistic economy 94

M
measure phrase 74

N
nominal classification *see* classifier
non-antecedent-based use of pro-forms 24, 76, 133–4. *See also* Abstract Construction; Human Construction
non-identity 24–5, 43, 49, 104, 130, 143
number 5, 12, 25, 27, 29, 39, 44–5, 48, 55–7, 59, 66, 68, 71, 84, 86, 106, 111, 115–16, 122–3, 127, 130–1, 134, 136–8, 140
number phrase 5, 27, 44–5, 66–7, 75, 134, 138
numeral: cardinal 6, 9–10, 17, 35, 38–9, 55, 57, 62, 71, 89, 96, 98, 134, 138, 140–1; ordinal 9–10, 29–30, 33, 37–8, 43, 46, 57–8, 63, 71

O
one as numeral 8, 11, 39, 62, 63

P
partitive construction 2, 26, 30, 33–4, 46, 60, 129
partitivity 21, 26–7, 30–9, 43, 47, 55, 58, 60, 80, 140–2
phonological deletion 19, 44, 46, 67, 69–83, 127, 130, 137, 138
pronominal forms 1, 19, 23, 25–7, 30, 32–3, 39, 50–2, 65, 67–9, 82–3, 91, 103, 118, 131, 134–5, 143; *pro*, 19, 25–30, 32–3, 35, 46, 79, 134
proper noun 67, 120, 122–3, 127

Q
quantifier 10, 13–14, 27, 29, 31, 36, 44, 54, 57, 59–60, 72, 79, 83, 96, 140–1
quantifier projection 5, 44, 45, 66–7

R
redundancy 29, 48, 70, 72, 75, 83, 94, 111, 125–6, 130
reference: coreference 23, 43, 50–4, 118, 130, 136, 143; generic 2, 52, 54, 72, 76–8, 81, 86, 116–17, 127, 131, 139–40; specific 31–3, 35, 52
restrictive modification 24, 36, 43, 53, 63

S
salience 12, 85, 94, 118, 124, 126, 132
specificity *see* reference
spoken language 3, 85, 90–5, 105, 113, 118, 126–7, 131, 135
stress 8, 40, 42, 54, 61–5, 118, 134–5, 137
substitution 1, 50
superlative 9, 11, 28, 37, 58, 63
Swedish 69

T
taxonomies 86, 95–8, 101, 104–19, 127, 131, 143
text type 113–14
Thai 44, 73
theta role 134

W
written language 3–4, 85, 91, 93, 95, 105, 113, 126–7, 131

X
X-bar syntax 4